Appletopia

Appletopia
Media Technology and the Religious
Imagination of **Steve Jobs**

Brett T. Robinson

BAYLOR UNIVERSITY PRESS

Cover design and custom illustration by Jeff Miller, Faceout Studio.
Book design by Diane Smith

Library of Congress Cataloging-in-Publication Data

Robinson, Brett T., 1975–
  Appletopia : media technology and the religious imagination of Steve Jobs / Brett T. Robinson, Baylor University Press.
  159 pages cm
  Includes bibliographical references and index.
  ISBN 978-1-60258-821-9 (hbk. : alk. paper)
  1. Social change. 2. Mass media—Technological innovations—Social aspects. 3. Mass media—Influence. 4. Jobs, Steve, 1955–2011. 5. Apple Computer, Inc. I. Title.
  HM831.R6293 2013
  302.23--dc23
                                      2013002241

Printed in the United States of America on acid-free paper with a minimum of 30% post-consumer-waste recycled content.

To my parents

Thomas E. Robinson
and
Aileen G. Robinson

and to Read Mercer Schuchardt, who started all this

The endless cycle of idea and action,
Endless invention, endless experiment,
Brings knowledge of motion, but not of stillness;
Knowledge of speech, but not of silence;
Knowledge of words, and ignorance of the Word.

—T. S. Eliot, "The Rock"

Now is the hour for us to rise from sleep.

—Romans 13:1

Contents

Acknowledgments

The idea that this project could become a book was born over a few Belgian beers on the west end of Pittsburgh. Among the many esteemed writers around the table at the Sharp Edge Creekhouse, I have Mike Aquilina, Craig Maier, Bob Lockwood, and David Scott to thank for cultivating a nascent interest in religion and technology, and Stephen R. Graham for putting me in touch with the fine folks at Baylor University Press.

Carey Newman, director at Baylor University Press, gave me a ten-month master class in writing that will remain with me forever. His use of metaphor to demystify the writing process is legendary and deserves its own book. Baylor's team of experts, who read and reread the manuscript and made sure everything on the business end ran smoothly, deserve great thanks and admiration.

The members of my doctoral committee who waded through the early drafts of this project deserve special thanks: Drs. Anandam Kavoori, Carolina Acosta-Alzuru, Janice Hume, Nathaniel Kohn, and Thomas Lessl. Thanks are due also to Dr. Scott Shamp, director of the University of Georgia New Media Institute, who kindled a fledgling fascination with new media. More importantly, Scott introduced me to my wife, which started my lifelong fascination with her.

Saint Vincent College kindly gave me the opportunity to teach a course on the topic of religion, technology, and marketing with an all-star lineup of students who became world-class research assistants: Trish Allan, Eric Arbore, Evan Lucas, Dan Hepple, Nick Mirando, Greta Edgar, Carli Ferretti, and Brendan Kucik.

Thanks also to Marlo Verrilla and Randi Senchur, whose tireless pursuit of interlibrary loan books, images, and citations was nothing short of tenacious.

Thanks to the dozens of Benedictine monks at Saint Vincent Archabbey who make the college such a grounded place to work, especially Brother Bruno Heisey, who curated a collection of delightful cartoons for my office door satirizing the sacred cows of technology.

Dr. John Sherry and the University of Notre Dame marketing faculty generously offered vital feedback in the final stages of the project, for which I am most grateful. It was an honor to present this work at my alma mater, where the seeds for these ideas were planted two decades ago.

Thanks to Dr. Michael Krom, a philosopher of the highest rank, who read an early draft of the manuscript and raised excellent questions that vastly improved the final product. Michael's appreciation for the finer things in life coupled with a true contemplative spirit is much needed in a world that has lost ears to hear and eyes to see. His students are very lucky, and I count myself among them.

This book was also the product of helpful conversations with Diane Montagna. Her patient ear, deep insights, and pitch-perfect wordsmithery were indispensable to the project.

Thanks to my immediate family, especially my sister Mandy Pond, my parents Tom and Aileen Robinson, and my late grandparents Bill and Madeline Gilroy and James and Helen Robinson. Your love and support over the years has made all of this possible.

Thanks are due as well to our neighbors David and Robin Klimke, John and Sharon Matz, Boomer and Barb Thompson, John and Sue

Bainbridge, and Jerome and Karen Foss for helping with the kids and celebrating all the little things life has to offer. They are all family.

Finally, my deepest thanks belong to my wife and children: thanks to Joseph, my three-year-old assistant, who kept me company in the writing "cave" during many long afternoons when he could have been playing outside. Thanks to John, my seven-year-old man, whose constant questioning fueled my own. Thanks to Anna, my baby girl, whose smile is nothing short of sublime.

I joked to my wife that writing a book was a little like having a baby: months and months of carrying the ideas around waiting for them to grow, lots of labor trying to get them out, and so on. It was only fitting then that we discovered our fourth child is due the same day this book will be released. Danielle, your generous spirit, your patience, and your grace have been inspirational. Thank you.

Apple Store, Fifth Avenue,
New York City

Introduction

Media Technology and Cultural Change

I n 2011 by one estimate the most photographed landmark in New York City was not Rockefeller Center or Times Square; it was the Apple Store on Fifth Avenue (see facing page).[1] The shimmering glass cube is otherworldly. The $7 million structure stands thirty-two feet high and features a glass spiral staircase wrapped around a glass elevator. A glowing Apple logo floats in the center of the cube. Inside the store, there are no shelves or boxes, just wooden tables with Apple's glowing products on display. Faithful consumers wander the cavernous interior admiring Apple devices in a virtual "cathedral of consumption."[2]

In his novel *Notre-Dame de Paris*, Victor Hugo's archdeacon looks up at the Notre-Dame Cathedral with a book in his hand and says, "This will kill that. The book will kill the edifice." Hugo explains the archdeacon's comment this way:

> It was a presentiment that human thought, in changing its form, was about to change its mode of expression; that the

dominant idea of each generation would no longer be written with the same matter, and in the same manner; that the book of stone, so solid and so durable, was about to make way for the book of paper, more solid and still more durable.[3]

The cultural authority of the cathedral was giving way to the revolution of ideas unleashed by the printing press and books.[4] Hugo's parable is instructive for the modern age as well. The authority of the printed page is now giving way to the universality of glass screens.

The transcendent design of the Apple store fits a historical pattern wherein the dominant media technology of an age acquires a sacred status (facing page, bottom).[5] The baroque design of the Library of Congress in Washington, D.C., and the vaulted ceiling of the Long Room in Trinity College Library in Dublin (facing page, top) are testaments to the sacred status granted to books as precious vessels of knowledge and cultural patrimony. When books were king, their homes were built in the highest architectural style of the day. Libraries were imagined as sacred spaces because they were instruments for transmitting culture to future generations, promoting community, and organizing chaos.[6]

The Apple Store is a shrine to the modern media technologies that now perform these tasks. Computers and smartphones have become tools for living as they have been integrated into nearly every facet of social and cultural life in the technological society. The durability of stone and paper is giving way to the ephemerality of bits and screens. Book and screen will continue to coexist, but our modes of expression are progressively beginning to favor the screen over the page. Patterns of thinking once routinized by the linear and logical flow of print are becoming more nonlinear and impressionistic by virtue of our heavy interaction with screen media and interactive technology.[7] We are beginning to think differently as a result of the new dominant media technologies.

The Apple Store also resembles La Grande Arche in Paris (see p. 4), a massive cube built to honor the secular humanitarian ideals of postwar France. La Grande Arche is large enough to fit the Notre-Dame

Long Room, Trinity College
Library, Dublin

Apple Store, Covent
Garden, London

La Grande Arche,
Paris

Cathedral inside its 348-foot-wide hollow center. La Grande Arche stands in stark contrast to the curvaceous Notre-Dame Cathedral, a baroque building representing old world tradition and fading cultural authority.[8] The modernist cube buttresses the sky, not with spires and gargoyles, but with precise lines and angles, a symbol of rational and disenchanted cultural aspirations. Despite their aesthetic contrast with the cathedrals of old, La Grande Arche and the Apple Store both represent a social order that is deemed inviolable, clothed with an aura of factuality, and vigorously maintained by its adherents.[9] Both monuments to modernism glorify technology and the secular ideals of the age.

Reading the Rhetoric of Technology

The beliefs and values of the technological age are embedded in a web of cultural relationships. The representation and practice of technology are composed of a diffuse set of rituals and rhetoric that resist tidy categorization.[10] Architecture provides a few clues about the beliefs and values of a particular age, but it is in the popular texts of the mass media that a more detailed picture emerges. The images and slogans of technology advertising provide a computer catechism of sorts, teaching the consumer the goods (and evils) of different products and services.[11] Just as the stained glass and statuary of medieval cathedrals educated converts and the illiterate, the iconic images and parables of advertising reveal the virtues of new technology to the buying public.[12]

The iconography of the Apple computer company provides a fitting case study for looking at the ways in which technology and the sacred have been conflated in the modern age. The Apple brand is the latest in a long line of American symbols that have captured the national imagination and spawned a "cult" of loyalists.[13] Well before Apple, the most photographed sites in the early twentieth century were places like the Grand Canyon and the Golden Gate Bridge, where tourists united in a collective sense of wonder and nationalism. Standing at the gaping mouth of the Grand Canyon evoked dread and awe, a mix of emotions that made for a sublime encounter.[14]

6   The sense that the world is charged with grandeur and mystery has largely faded in the wake of a dogmatic deference to rationalism in the modern world. As a result, the world has lost some of its primordial magic.[15] Thus, an electrifying encounter with a technological wonder reinvests the world with a transcendent significance. In a country with divergent religious views, these collective moments of wonder provide an important social bond.[16]

One of America's great industrial feats, the Golden Gate Bridge, was an answer to the problem of isolation and disconnect. Suspended in the air, the bridge spans an immense physical divide, connecting two cities and millions of people. The bridge is a tremendous feat of art and engineering that fuels a collective faith in our ability to harness technology to overcome the chasms that separate humanity. Communication technologies work in much the same way. The metaphysical space that separates individuals is viewed as an obstacle to more empathic relationships and social cohesion. The imaginary bridges we build with media technologies seem to move us toward a more perfect communion.[17] A noble aspiration to be sure, but it may not be true.

The orientation of personal technology is like its name, highly personal—directed toward the individual rather than the collective. It has led to what the famed sociologist of religion Emile Durkheim called the "cult of the individual."[18] Durkheim saw the cult of the individual on the horizon as a strong theoretical possibility given the speed with which rationalization was draining religion of its power to provide a meaningful social bond. Transcendence was no longer something to be sought "out there." The sacred relocated to the subjective experience of the individual. With the advent of personal technologies—symbols of radical individualism realized—the theory appears to have some value.[19]

The cult of Apple is shorthand for the devotion of Apple technology enthusiasts, but their fidelity and fervor point to a more fundamental link between the cult of technology and the cult of the individual. Apple founder Steve Jobs is an allegorical figure for reading the ways in which technology and individual value systems intersect to produce an implicit religion.[20] Technology, like religion, becomes a site where the physical and the metaphysical meet. The promotion of modern technology revives dreams of communion brought on by networked information. The objects that transmit ephemeral bits of culture, promote virtual community, and organize the digital chaos have become sacred objects. Jesus Martín-Barbero puts it this way:

> Despite all the promise of modernity to make religion disappear, what has really happened is that religion has modernized itself. . . . What we are witnessing is not the conflict of religion and modernity, but the transformation of modernity into enchantment by linking new communication technologies to the logic of popular religiosity.[21]

The roots of technological faith can be found, ironically enough, in the romanticism of the mid-nineteenth century, a contemplative response to the technological and spiritual changes wrought by the Industrial Revolution.[22] Nineteenth-century American art and poetry echoed a romantic spirit of perfectibility and spiritual encounter between the virgin wilderness and the individual soul. Transcendentalists like Ralph Waldo Emerson and Henry David Thoreau believed that religious institutions corrupted individual purity, and so they sought a self-reliant spirituality divorced of creeds and dogmas.[23] Modern ideas about monism have their roots in this American romanticism, a spiritual reflection of democratic ideals and the sacred status of the individual in early American political thought. As railroads and telegraph lines transformed the natural landscape, the language of transcendence began to adopt technological metaphors. Emerson saw the new technologies as expressions of a new metaphysical view: "Our civilization and these ideas are reducing the earth to a brain. See how by telegraph and steam the Earth is anthropologized."[24]

A century later, technology theorists like Teilhard de Chardin would revive Emerson's vision in the form of the noosphere, an idea that Earth was evolving toward a superconsciousness by virtue of

8   electronic communication.[25] The rhetoric of technology that emerged from the foment of the 1960s counterculture described a new nature that married the metaphysical and the technological. The 1967 poem "All Watched Over by Machines of Loving Grace" by Richard Brautigan combined computers with utopian aspirations: "I like to think / (it has to be!) / of a cybernetic ecology / where we are free of our labors / and joined back to nature, / returned to our mammal brothers and sisters, / and all watched over / by machines of loving grace."[26] At the heart of the countercultural movement was something vaguely spiritual—a desire for more perfect communion with nature and with one another, a new consciousness.[27]

The coupling of technology and romanticism, science and spirituality, has fostered what American sociologist Philip Rieff has called "the triumph of the therapeutic."[28] Under these conditions, the moral ideal is a person of leisure, "released by technology from the regimental discipline of work so as to secure his sense of well-being in highly refined alloplastic ways."[29] The high priests of such an age appear in the form of media icons like Oprah Winfrey, doctors turned mystics like Deepak Chopra, and technology gurus like Steve Jobs. Each of these celebrities supports the cult of the individual by offering psychological and technological salvation to a disenchanted world.[30]

Technology has not always inspired loving grace and flights of spiritual fancy, however. The Luddite movement of the early nineteenth century in England saw textile workers engage in the destruction of mechanized looms in protest of the encroaching automation of labor. The Luddites feared for their livelihood as the Industrial Revolution introduced labor-saving machines that made many workers expendable.[31] Such a dramatic change to a centuries-old way of life was a shock to the economic and cultural system and sowed the seeds for the romantic movement. It was art and poetry that rescued humans from their conflict with machines by invoking an escape into nature. Apple's Steve Jobs believed that combining art and technology would release people from the old antagonisms. The Apple narrative inspired by Jobs is mythic in its ability to reimagine technology, not as a dehumanizing force, but as something liberating and natural.

Vehicles of Transcendence

The history of Silicon Valley provides a fitting backdrop for reading the American religion of technology. When Steve Jobs set up shop in his parents' garage to start work on the first Apple computer, a significant cultural shift was under way. Prior to the personal computer, the machine of highest rank in the great chain of automation was the automobile.[32]

At the dawn of the information revolution, it was the car, not the computer, that signaled the coming shift in consciousness that would transform the American landscape. In the early 1900s, the El Camino Real corridor of California was home to dozens of mission churches built by Spanish Franciscan friars to convert and evangelize the Native Americans of the region. The churches were beautiful, built in the Spanish mission style, and they brought a sense of old world mystique to a region that would end up being defined by innovation and technology.

Eventually the glory of the mission churches faded as California became ripe for development. Like those of most states in the early twentieth century, the California landscape was being remapped by the highway system to make way for the automobile. A sampling of tourist photos from the 1920s shows a steady stream of travelers stopping for photo ops in front of the missions with their cars positioned prominently in the foreground.[33] The trip up the California coast, with the infinite expanse of the ocean on one side and portals to the divine on the other, was a motorist's dream, a way of escaping the everyday. It became one of the most popular automobile tours on the continent.

Tucked into the northern leg of the El Camino Real is the present-day Silicon Valley. Bordered by the Santa Clara Mission, Silicon Valley is sacred ground for those invested in the culture of digital technology. The transformation of El Camino Real from religious-automotive pilgrimage to mecca of modern technology is an allegory for the digital age. It reveals our manic desire for transcendence and all of the means by which we seek it, from religion to cars to computers. Churches, cars, and computers share a secret affinity. They help us escape. The really special ones are works of art. Chartres, Ferrari, and the iPod are all cathedrals—each one transporting us in different ways.[34]

It is fitting then that the Apple computer—the machine that would become the icon of technological sophistication in the information age—was born in a garage. In December 1980, the Apple computer company went public, and the success of the stock offering eclipsed the previous record-setting offering by Ford Motor in 1956.[35] In retrospect, this fact is not surprising given the industrial heights to which Apple would eventually ascend. But Apple and Ford are linked by more than their monetary success and iconic status.

Cars and computers are built to transport the user—one moves the body and the other moves the mind. Both machines changed our relationship to space and time. Automotive transport necessitated the suburb and the superhighway. American maps had to be completely redrawn to record the vast network of highway and byway arteries that became the nation's circulatory system. Not to be outdone, the growth of electronic communication gave the country a nervous system.[36] Not only could people and materials be transported at high speeds, speech and image could be transmitted at the speed of light. The country was linked by telegraph, telephone, radio, television, and then computer. Private and mobile transcendent experiences were being realized as both cars and computers overcame physical limits.

The communication revolution inspired a slew of sublime rhetoric. In the early days of the personal computer, Nicholas Negroponte of the MIT Media Lab waxed prophetically that our world would be irrevocably changed by the immateriality of bits replacing the materiality of atoms.[37] With the growing popularity of ebooks and the slow death of print newspapers, Negroponte's predictions echoed the prophecy of Victor Hugo's archdeacon in *Notre-Dame de Paris*, "this will kill that." Negroponte's rhetoric of digital technology bears the traces of ancient gnostic yearnings to escape the bonds of physical materiality to become one with sacred knowledge, or gnosis.[38]

This pattern of rhetorical transference between the technological and the transcendent has found ample purchase in the Apple story. With Apple and Steve Jobs, the sibling relationship between technology and transcendence is writ large. Apple's religiosity has been attributed to everything from the company's "forbidden fruit" logo to the fervent devotion of Apple consumers who make pilgrimages to Apple stores and defend the brand against the heresies of Microsoft. However, the company's evocative symbols and devoted users are symptomatic of a much deeper transformation at work in the culture.

The Greek word *metanoia* is helpful in thinking about the transformation in consciousness at work in the digital age. The term is usually associated with religious conversion, but the literal meaning of *metanoia* (μετάνοια) is "radical change of thought and mind."[39] In 1997 Steve Jobs staked the future of the beleaguered Apple computer company on a similar idea—a grammatically suspect two-word phrase, "Think Different." The advertising slogan was an instant hit and became the centerpiece of a promotional campaign for Apple that coincided with the explosive growth of the commercial Internet. The personal computer went from being an object for specialists to a necessary household appliance. The world was beginning to think differently, and Jobs was leading the way. In the spirit of his romantic forebears like Emerson, Jobs imagined the computer as a metaphor for the human mind:

> Our minds are sort of electrochemical computers. Your thoughts construct patterns like scaffolding in your mind. You are really etching chemical patterns. In most cases, people get stuck in those patterns, just like grooves in a record, and they never get out of them. It's a rare person who etches grooves that are other than a specific way of looking at things, a specific way of questioning things. It's rare that you see an artist in his 30s or 40s able to really contribute something amazing.

Of course, there are some people who are innately curious, forever little kids in their awe of life, but they're rare.[40]

The chemical patterns etched by the habitual use of personal technology are changing the way we think, act, and feel. As a result, cultural practices like religion are beginning to change as well. When religious ideas were locked away in monasteries and printed on manuscripts, religious authority was centralized. The printing press democratized religious interpretation and put religious texts into the hands of many. The mass production and distribution of theological, philosophical, and scientific ideas was a watershed moment that remapped the intellectual and spiritual landscape of the West.[41] In the age of the personal computer, popular religious positions have become even more diffuse—a symptom of the powerful and personalized technologies we use to communicate.

The computer is more decentralized than are printed books. Tim Berners-Lee, lead architect of the World Wide Web, noted the parallels between his Unitarian Universalist faith and the decentralized architecture of the web, designed to encourage tolerance and a mutual search for truth.[42] The ethic of the Internet age is rooted in free expression, a breakdown of hierarchy, a sense of individual empowerment, and a distrust of central authority. Each of these developments poses a threat to traditional religious institutions. It should be no surprise that religious participation has faltered rather than flourished since the birth of the television and the computer.[43] This is not to say that technology is the only factor in the erosion of religious influence, but the correspondence of the two trends is more than coincidence.

The void left by fading religious authorities and the ethic instilled by technology use may favor a more libertarian approach to spirituality and belief, but the desire for transcendence persists. When the shared sense of transcendence recedes from the wonders of nature and the baroque cathedrals of religion, enchantment is sought elsewhere. Digital images of the sublime, from the Grand Canyon to the outer reaches of the cosmos, now live on computer desktops and screen savers as constant reminders of the human desire to see beyond the blandness of routinized work. The computer provides a mode of escape and an invitation to dwell in an alternative universe of imagery and information.

Media Metaphors and Religious Rhetoric

Education and catechism in the technological religion extend into all areas of cultural life. Children are introduced to communication technologies in the home at a very early age. The millennia it took for man to move from oral communication to print communication to electronic communication have been condensed to a few years for the young initiate. Once the initiate is in school, the educational environment provides further training in computers and media literacy. By high school, many children are outfitted with laptops purchased by the school. The ritual use of computers and cell phones by young people places them in "imagined communities" where relationships consist of text messaging, email, and sharing other bits of media.[44]

The use of cell phones, laptops, and tablets has skyrocketed over the past decade, and the trends show no signs of slowing down. Americans spend between eight and nine hours a day in front of some type of screen. While the television still accounts for the bulk of screen time among Americans, the computer and mobile devices are quickly encroaching. Among eighteen- to forty-four-year-olds, the combined time spent with computers and mobile devices is nearly equal to television screen time.[45] As screen time increases, the character of social and cultural life changes.[46]

A Latin phrase is frequently repeated in the Catholic Church: *lex orandi, lex credendi, lex vivendi*, which can be translated, "how we worship reflects what we believe and determines how we will live."[47] In the age of screen worship, media technology has become a determinant of contemplative habits (or lack thereof). Apple's Steve Jobs was fond of the Hindu saying, "In the first 30 years of your life, you make your habits. For the last 30 years of your life, your habits make

14   you."[48] Jobs had it printed on invitations to his thirtieth birthday party. The phrase was prescient. Over the next two decades, the technology products Apple created became a global obsession. Jobs' habits changed the world.

The word "habit" comes from the religious apparel worn by clerical orders of monks and nuns. It also means a "customary practice." The iPods worn by millions of Apple devotees are both apparel and habitual practice. The popularity of listening to digital music, reading electronic books, and browsing the Internet on cell phones is due in large part to Jobs' inspiration.

Apple devices encourage self-expression by inviting spontaneous creativity and personalization. The ads for the Apple iPod are icons of ecstatic self-expression, as silhouetted dancers let loose in fits of choreographed glee, their bodies coordinated with the rhythm of the music supplied by their iPod devices (see p. 44 for an example). The faceless shadows that float on psychedelic backgrounds in the iPod ads connote a spiritual happening. The music affects both body and soul. The ability of the iPod ads to evoke religious comparison is a product of their highly metaphorical presentation.

Religious communication uses metaphorical language because it proposes realities that cannot be grasped directly. The invisible workings of the metaphysical realm are understood in relation to something sensible and concrete. Religion is communicated through stories, symbols, art, and analogies. The parables in the gospel are common tales of farmers, day laborers, and landowners. Images of fruitful seeds, just wages, and merciful fathers reveal facets of an infinite God to the finite mind. The Buddhist concept of *dukkha* (suffering) is a metaphorical term that translates as "bad wheel." The Buddha compared suffering to the bad wheel of an oxcart that makes for an unsteady and uncomfortable ride. The use of metaphor in religious rhetoric makes the metaphysical sensible.

The rhetoric of technology resembles religion in its need for metaphors to make the unknown sensible.[49] It is why the steam engine was first explained in terms of horsepower rather than a physics equation.

Thanks to artistic engineers like Jobs, computers are filled with easy-to-understand metaphors: folders, desktops, icons, and memory to name just a few. Part of Jobs' genius was finding the metaphors that resonated with the uninitiated user. While a term like subdirectory meant very little to the average user, putting a file in a folder made perfect sense. Making the computer interface visual and image-based rather than text-based made the experience of personal computing accessible to those who were not computer literate.

The education of the illiterate through the use of metaphors and visual icons bears a resemblance to the experience of medieval churchgoers who relied on iconography, stained glass, and cathedral architecture to provide instruction on the core tenets of the faith.[50] Italian cultural critic and semiotician Umberto Eco made the connection between the metaphors of religion and technology in a famous essay in which he described "a new underground religious war which is modifying the modern world."[51] Eco's tongue-in-cheek metaphor goes like this: The Apple Macintosh computer is Catholic and Microsoft Windows/DOS is Protestant. Macintosh is Catholic because it is "counter-reformist and has been influenced by the ratio studiorum of the Jesuits. It is cheerful, friendly, conciliatory; it tells the faithful how they must proceed step by step to reach—if not the kingdom of Heaven—the moment in which their document is printed. It is catechistic: The essence of revelation is dealt with via simple formulae and sumptuous icons. Everyone has a right to salvation."

The DOS machine is Protestant because "it allows free interpretation of scripture, demands difficult personal decisions, imposes a subtle hermeneutics upon the user, and takes for granted the idea that not all can achieve salvation. To make the system work you need to interpret the program yourself: Far away from the baroque community of revelers, the user is closed within the loneliness of his own inner torment." His analysis also includes the improvements made by Microsoft to upgrade DOS to Windows. Eco notes, "Windows represents an Anglican-style schism, big ceremonies in the cathedral, but there is always the possibility of a return to DOS to change things in accordance with bizarre decisions: When it comes down to it, you can decide to ordain women and gays if you want to." Eco's satirical approach reveals the compatibility of religious and technological metaphors. This was not lost on Steve Jobs, who approached new technology with the zeal of a prophet. Undeterred by social critics who saw computers as an expression of dehumanization in the modern age,[52] Jobs saw creativity and life in the cold, beige machines that were taking over corporate cubicles and military installations. Within a decade of starting the Apple computer company in his garage, Steve Jobs staged an ideological battle with computer manufacturing giant IBM over what it meant to be human in the age of machines.

Inspired by a sense of spiritual purpose, Steve Jobs warned that an unchallenged IBM would usher in a dark age in which bleak boxes of microchips would turn workers into mindless drones. Jobs flipped the script by imagining computers as mystical tools for unleashing human creative potential. Jobs' vision of machines as spiritual liberators was enshrined in the famous 1984 advertisement depicting IBM as George Orwell's Big Brother and Apple as the rebellious hero smashing the shibboleths of the IBM computer culture.

The story of our love/hate relationship with technology is best told by the artists. Man and technology are two actors involved in a timeless story about the response of the creator to the created. This is the stuff of myth, poetry, legend, and religion. Adam and Eve, Prometheus, and Frankenstein's monster all speak to the dreadful and intoxicating proposition of playing God. And it is the sense of dread and overwhelming mystery that evokes the sublime. The sublime can be both a religious sensation and a technological one. In the technological age, it is not just the poets and painters who present the transcendent but the engineers and programmers as well.

Advertising has been dubbed the "official art" of capitalist society, and rightly so. Advertising is more than persuasive rhetoric; it is an aesthetic encounter. The mode of persuasion in advertising is not always rational; it is highly emotive.[53] Evocative images, music, and the physical design and contours of a product are seductive; they call upon our sensuality. In the modern cultural climate, where product art is more influential and pervasive than fine art, the proliferation of values and taste changes. Fine art represents human longing by depicting what we believe is true and good and beautiful. In the world of product art we receive a distorted view of the true, the good, and the beautiful. We are shown material goods that are beautified, and we are told that the promises they make are true.

Our ideas about the true, the good, and the beautiful come from religious belief. If advertising parodies such metaphysical ideals, then it is also taking a swipe at religion. Such parody is evident in everything from Angel Soft toilet paper to Miracle Whip. The fallout from this semantic hijacking changes the way religion is perceived.[54] Religious traditions are raided for symbols and narratives to enhance the appeal of commodities. When those symbols are abstracted from their traditions and used for other purposes, they are drained of their primordial potency. In certain cases, the products and brands themselves take on a religious significance.

The reciprocal use of technological and religious metaphor has led to some imaginative rhetoric over the centuries. Steve Jobs and the Apple computer company embody the blending of technology and religion metaphors remarkably well; they offer a curious mix of the technical and the transcendental, the mechanical and the mystical, the technological and the theological. From Jobs' esoteric Buddhism to the Apple consumers who proudly declare their membership in the Apple cult, the commingling of religion and technology in the Apple story is a reflection of a persistent and fascinating cultural preoccupation. A society's most popular technologies provide the all-important metaphors for articulating spiritual concerns. As such, Steve Jobs and the Apple computer company provide hieroglyphs for understanding the sibling relationship between technology and the sacred in the computer age.

The advertisements for the Apple computer company are emblems of a culture that has adopted technology as a de facto religion, a

18   religion that celebrates the cult of the individual. Media devices are
the means by which we communalize our concerns and ritualize the
practice of self-divinization by procuring the powers of omniscience
and omnipresence granted by a global communication network. Personal computers, music players, and cell phones fashion us votaries of
the digital age, and Apple has imagined our technological conversion
in compelling ways. Apple's advertisements provide a rich visual allegory for reading the transference of spiritual and technological desire
in the digital age.

1

Macintosh Myths

Allegories for the Information Age

When Steve Jobs introduced the Macintosh computer in a California auditorium in 1984, he looked more like a university professor than a hippie turned computer impresario. Dressed in a green bow tie and dark blazer, he announced to the audience, "All the images you are about to see on the large screen will be generated by what's in that bag." In a grandiloquent gesture, Jobs pulled a small diskette from his jacket pocket to cheers from the audience. The song "Chariots of Fire" played over the loudspeakers as the word "MACINTOSH" scrolled slowly across the screen to wild cheers from the audience.

What a strange spectacle: the antics of a quirky computer salesman and the graphics of a nine-inch monochrome display whipping an audience of thousands into a frenzy. The moment was a testament to Jobs' infectious enthusiasm. It also signaled a paradigm shift in computing. The Macintosh launch reimagined the computer as a tool for creative expression and individual freedom after decades of being a symbol of cold computation.[1]

20   Jobs believed that computing was more than crunching code; it was supposed to be an aesthetic and artistic experience as well. Jobs remembered, "I always thought of myself as a humanities person as a kid, but I liked electronics. Then I read something that one of my heroes, Edwin Land of Polaroid, said about the importance of people who could stand at the intersection of humanities and sciences, and I decided that's what I wanted to do."[2] The images displayed at the 1984 Macintosh launch alternated between sketches of classical architecture and computer code, between spreadsheets and image editing software. The Macintosh married left brain and right brain. In fact, it seemed to have a mind of its own. At one point, Jobs asked the computer to say a few words, and the Macintosh responded with some humorous quips about never trusting a computer you can't lift (IBM) and how Steve Jobs has been like a father figure to the Macintosh. The machine born during the Cold War had a creative pulse.[3]

In the course of Jobs' presentation of the new Macintosh, the screen displayed a photo of Steve Jobs. It was an iconic moment in the introduction of the new computer. At one level, it was merely a way of demonstrating the computer's graphics capabilities. At another level, it revealed an important dimension of the human-computer dynamic. To see oneself in a creation is the ultimate expression of one's creative spirit. Jobs, the demiurge of digital culture, was creating technology in his own image and likeness.

Gnosticism in "1984"

Apple's early advertising avoided esoteric language about bits and processors and instead focused on constructing a mythical framework for imagining personal computing.[4] Apple produced their famous "1984" ad to launch the first Macintosh during the 1984 Super Bowl.[5] There are no Macintosh computers in the ad, and the Apple logo does not appear until the very end. Instead, the ad shows a dreary, dystopian science fiction scene in which an army of expressionless drones stare, mouths agape, at a large screen broadcasting an Orwellian rant about ideology and control. The figure on the screen can be interpreted as representing Apple's competitor IBM. The portrayal is meant to evoke the figure of Big Brother from Orwell's novel *1984*, a not so subtle play on IBM's nickname, Big Blue. The imposing figure on the screen barks out a caustic monologue:

> Today we celebrate the first glorious anniversary of the Information Purification Directives. We have created for the first time in all history a garden of pure ideology, where each worker may bloom, secure from the pests of any contradictory true thoughts. Our Unification of Thoughts is more powerful a weapon than any fleet or army on earth. We are one people, with one will, one resolve, one cause. Our enemies shall talk themselves to death and we will bury them with their own confusion. We shall prevail!

The climax of the ad occurs when a woman, who is being pursued by armed guards, runs into the middle of the assembly and hurls a sledgehammer at the giant screen. The resulting explosion releases a burst of light that washes over the indoctrinated masses while a voiceover reads the text crawl, "On January 24th Apple Computer will introduce Macintosh. And you'll see why 1984 won't be like '1984.' "

The advertisement contrasts a totalitarian vision of technology with the liberating power of Macintosh. Liberation is portrayed as an individual exercise, one performed in the face of great social pressure to assimilate to a dreary, mechanistic mode of existence. The woman is young, strong, and rebellious; an image in sync with the budding feminist philosophies of the mid-1980s that questioned male dominance, especially in the realm of technology.[6] Perhaps most striking is the visual of the explosion as the woman's sledgehammer destroys the screen displaying the ominous male figure. The screen does not explode in typical Hollywood fashion with orange balls of fire and black smoke. Instead, the catastrophic event releases a dazzling torrent of white light that illuminates the darkened hall and transfixes the individuals in attendance. Awakened from their hypnotic state, the men gaze with mouths hanging open, overwhelmed by dread and awe.

Apple commemorative poster, "1984"

seated figures, "1984"

The symbolism of the blinding white light in "1984" provides early evidence of Apple's propensity to dabble in metaphysical themes when promoting products (see p. 22). Specifically, Apple's advertising symbolism draws upon a gnostic sensibility. The following passage from gnostic scripture aligns well with the "awakening" scene in the "1984" ad:

> They bestowed upon the guardians a sublime call, to shake up and make to rise those that slumber. They were to awaken the souls that had stumbled away from the place of light. They were to awaken them and shake them up, that they might lift their faces to the place of light.[7]

The female Macintosh revolutionary is a figure for "self-divinization" —a process by which the gnostic, through her own magical and intellectual labor, achieves gnosis, a share in the mind of God. In the mythos of technology, the seemingly infinite body of knowledge offered by the computer puts us in touch with a sense of omniscience.

The polysemous text of the ad also suggests a reading of the cult of drones as the figures in Plato's cave who have not yet seen the divine light of wisdom, leading them to believe that the shadows on the wall are reality itself. The allegory is especially relevant today. Technology users gaze for hours a day at shadows on the screen. The images on-screen are reflections of reality, but not reality itself. They are digital shadows. For Plato and Socrates, it was contemplation and philosophy that would lead the prisoner to the light. In the Apple mythology, ironically enough, it is the personal computer. It is both the disease and the cure.

In the Western philosophical tradition, Neoplatonic ideas were linked to religious belief systems like Gnosticism.[8] Media scholar Erik Davis notes the way in which the rhetoric of technologists bears a distinct gnostic sensibility. In gnostic belief, the material body is a prison and the only way out is to attain the mystical enlightenment that gnosis or divine knowledge provides. The only way to achieve gnosis is to become like the gods and reclaim the divine knowledge lost in

24 the fall. An allegorical reading of the "1984" ad suggests this gnostic ideal in figurative terms. The heroine releases the masses from their material prison by using the giant hammer, a symbol of physical work and toil, as a weapon against the material regime. Her superhuman effort smashes the illusions broadcast by the authoritarian screen and releases the preternatural light.

Strains of Gnosticism can also be found in a reading of the Apple logo itself. The official story is that Steve Jobs worked on an apple commune in the 1970s and felt like it would be a good name for his fledgling computer company. He thought it would minimize the intimidation people felt around computers. When graphic designer Rob Janoff designed the current Apple logo, he added the bite to the side; otherwise, Jobs said it looked too much like a cherry tomato. Those may be the facts of the logo's creation, but the logo story that has persisted among Apple fans is far more mythological. Given Apple's penchant for the grandiose, how can one not read the bitten apple as the fruit from the tree of knowledge of good and evil in Genesis?

A documentary about Apple fanatics called *Macheads* captures a scene where two Apple fans are camping out on a New York City street, waiting in line to buy the new iPhone. Their conversation suddenly turns philosophical as they start to question why they are camping in the midst of New York City in the middle of the night to buy a phone. One gentleman says to the other,

> It was eating an apple that caused us as a race of people to be cast out of paradise. So maybe that same knowledge that was so evil early on in mankind's story remains evil and each time we take a bite of this technological "Apple," we move further from the garden that was our home and deeper into the hell that is our current want.[9]

The conventional interpretation of the Genesis account of creation is that Adam and Eve are beguiled by a serpent that tricks them into eating the forbidden fruit from the tree of knowledge of good and evil.

The serpent's pitch is that they will "be as gods, knowing good and evil." When they decided to partake, they cursed the rest of humanity with the burden of original sin, punishable by death and suffering. The gnostics read the story differently—in a way that makes for a much less forbidding take on the Apple logo with a bite removed.

According to the gnostics, death and suffering are not humanity's punishment for disobedience, but rather the state of a world created by a bumbling demiurge. In one of Gnosticism's sacred texts, the Secret Book of John, it is Christ who enters the garden, plays the part of the serpent, and offers the divine knowledge. By partaking, humans achieve gnosis and share in the divine knowledge.[10] Biting the apple was an act of liberation, not an occasion for condemnation. The rest of human history then is the story of those who attain the secret knowledge and those who do not.

Technology presents a similar dualism. There are the haves and have-nots—those who have access to technology and those who do not. There are the enlightened individuals who imbibe the creative spirit of Apple and the ignorant masses who choose otherwise and remain in the soulless dark. The symbol of the omniscient mind fits squarely within the information technology mythology. For Apple, the symbolism could not have been more ripe. Apple's implicit allegory about computers offering a secret knowledge appeals to a society in which self-actualization is tied to technological sophistication.[11]

In 1984 it would have been hard to predict the extent to which personal technology would transform the social and cultural landscape. Apple's over-the-top cinematic take on the coming revolution proved to be prescient. Computers shape daily interactions, from education to entertainment to shopping to banking to socializing. More important, computers shape "mental life."[12] For centuries, books had shaped the interior or mental life, objects that when opened speak of another consciousness, a rational being who communicates thoughts, ideas, and images to the engaged reader. The reader enters the book, and the book enters the reader.

26   Computers utilize metaphors of the page to encourage familiarity and ease of use. Eminent computer scientist and former Apple employee Alan Kay said this about the computer interface:

> By moving the page from book to screen, a new dynamic emerges: the screen as "paper to be marked on" is a metaphor that suggests pencils, brushes, and typewriting. . . . Should we transfer the paper metaphor so perfectly that the screen is as hard as paper to erase and change? Clearly not. If it is to be like magical paper, then it is the magical part that is all important.[13]

Unlike the page, the screen interface is one of illusion—an ephemeral grouping of electrons that can change or disappear at any moment. The intimacy of interacting with the sensory elements of the printed page, the combed texture, the smell of aged pulp, the crinkling of paper, is absent. As such, the "mental life" fostered by computers is one of fleeting relationships and sensory deprivation. It suggests an entirely different way of thinking about our relationship to the thoughts and imagination of others.

Enlightened Beings

The subtle changes in mental life that followed the adoption of personal computers were not lost on Steve Jobs. In fact, he staked Apple's future on two words that reflected the changing environment, "Think Different." Like most creative spirits, Jobs had a mercurial disposition, and his harsh management style became untenable for a company that was seeking stability. After a series of major disagreements with Apple management in the mid-1980s, the tempestuous Jobs spent a decade in exile while the company he founded lost its creative soul. Jobs' Odyssean return to Apple in 1997 signaled a rebirth for the moribund company.

    To commemorate Jobs' heroic return, the company launched the "Think Different" ad campaign (see facing page for an example). The

28   campaign featured famous personalities who captured the Apple spirit
of rebellious creativity. The wistful montage of black and white images
in the television ad included Albert Einstein, Bob Dylan, Gandhi,
Ted Turner, Picasso, and Muhammad Ali, among others. According
to the ad copy, they were the misfits, rebels, and troublemakers who
also changed the world. They were the "crazy ones" whose ability to
think differently was the mark of genius. The ad was a manifesto for
Apple's values.[14]

> Here's to the crazy ones. The misfits. The rebels. The trouble-
> makers. The round pegs in the square holes. The ones who see
> things differently. They're not fond of rules. And they have no
> respect for the status quo. You can quote them, disagree with
> them, glorify or vilify them. About the only thing you can't
> do is ignore them. Because they change things. They push the
> human race forward. While some may see them as the crazy
> ones, we see genius. Because the people who are crazy enough
> to think they can change the world, are the ones who do.

Jobs once quipped that some of the people in the "Think Different" ad
may not be alive, but if they were they would use Apple computers.[15]
Combining images of John Lennon and Gandhi with a brand focused
on pixels and gigahertz endowed the machine with a creative soul. In
an age increasingly characterized by disenchantment and the loss of
transcendence, the ad represented the marriage of hope and humanity
with technology. Apple computers were more than metal and glass,
they were body and spirit. They were the men and women of the
"Think Different" ad: Albert Einstein, Amelia Earhart, and Gandhi all
rolled into one. Jobs' friend Andy Hertzfeld said that Jobs would often
talk of people like Einstein and Gandhi as rare examples of enlightened beings. "Once," Hertzfeld recalls, "[Jobs] even hinted to me that
he was enlightened."[16]

The "Think Different" manifesto was an expression of Jobs' personal belief that the world was inhabited by enlightened beings and
that those beings were ambassadors of a higher consciousness.[17] For

Jobs, it was the world that was crazy—not the venerated individuals who knew how to think different. After returning from a pilgrimage to India in his early adulthood, Jobs was taken by the difference in thought patterns between East and West. The Indian villagers he met were much more intuitive than Westerners he knew. Many of the villagers were not literate, but they seemed to possess more wisdom. Jobs experienced culture shock when he returned to the West, where linear rationality ruled. The absence of intuition was troubling to Jobs, and he came to see the Western mind as deranged.[18]

The "Think Different" ad honors individual human potential, the ethos at the heart of American romanticism. In the Jobs mythology, enlightened beings were not the products of churches or governments, they were enlightened artists and iconoclasts who rejected tradition and embraced their own intuition. "Think Different" was an allegory for the coming age.[19] Technology offered a share in the creative resurgence of human potential, but it also required assimilation to the machines that make such a transformation possible.[20]

"I think, therefore iMac"

Shortly after the "Think Different" campaign, Apple released the iMac computer. The iMac was the next-generation Macintosh optimized for the Internet (hence the "i" prefix). The trope found most often in the iMac narrative is the personification of the computer. The aim of the messaging was to minimize the boundary between man and machine and imagine the computer as an extension of our own faculties. Jobs told one observer, "Deep inside every human being there is a source of creativity. A computer should be the extension of the creative human being."[21]

In the Mac narrative, differences in operating systems represent differences in cognition styles. Associating with a particular brand then is an affiliation not just with a name or corporate philosophy but with a way of thinking. The operating system is a metaphor for the mind.[22] A March 1999 print ad titled "I think, therefore iMac" is a

30   satire of Enlightenment philosopher René Descartes' famous phrase, "I think, therefore I am." The humor in the ad belies the implicit argument that computer technology relies on metaphors of human cognition.[23] By substituting "iMac" for "I am," the ad sets up a similitude between thinking and computing. It also suggests an existential statement about being in the information age. Owning a personal computer that connects to the Internet affirms my being in the digital world. The ad and the computer reflect the way we process information. The extent to which we prefer one interface over another reveals a cognitive predisposition. An insult hurled at PC users is not just about the type of computer they use, but an attack on their structure of thinking. Computer choice is a reflection of one's personality and way of looking at the world. The ability for a product like the iMac to possess personality traits or to reflect a particular way of thinking and processing information grants it a human likeness.

Narcissus Goes Shopping

Advertisements that reinforce the personification of iMac are numerous. In many cases, the ads do more than personify the computer. Like the "Think Different" ad, Macintosh ads also contain nostalgic signifiers that link the machine to familiar cultural symbols and practices.[24] One particularly iconic example involves a black male window shopping on a city street. He encounters a solitary iMac, bathed in white light, sitting in a shop window. In the background, a smokestack belches smoke into the evening air. Two streetlamps are visible, but the scene remains very dark. The monitor of the iMac turns to follow the man as he passes the window.[25] The man notices the computer moving on its own and stops to look (see facing page).

    The shop window motif recalls the industrial era's use of window displays to encourage consuming gazes from passers-by.[26] The darkness of the city street and the absence of a crowd suggest the window-shopping heyday has passed. The holiday displays, still-life scenes, and skillfully arranged products from shop windows of yesteryear

iMac ad campaign

32   are replaced by the solitary machine. The metaphor of the window display is appropriate for the new iMac, a machine known as much for its unique style as its processing power. The shop window also works as a nostalgic signifier in an age in which the television and computer screen are our windows to the world. The cultural practice of window shopping has largely disappeared as retailers increasingly move to online venues. Window shopping now takes place virtually on the computer. Consumers visit websites with products displayed in photographs and videos. In this way, the setup of the "Window" ad is synonymous with the function of the product. Computers provide a virtual "window shopping" experience as consumers sample the multitude of online offerings as if strolling through a city. The personal computer offers a gateway to virtual spectacles that render the physical city and the store window archaic.

Cultural critic Walter Benjamin's study of the Paris arcades in the early 1900s is helpful in interpreting the scene in the iMac ad. The Paris arcades were early iterations of the shopping mall, elegantly adorned shops displaying baubles and enticements that eventually fell into ruin. Benjamin was infatuated with the ruins of material culture because, from his theological-political view, ruins were the stuff of allegory. The arcades were "the original temple of commodity capitalism," and "they beamed out into the Paris of the second Empire like fairy grottoes."[27] The fairy grotto of the iMac window, with its glimmering white light and spritelike computer, enchants the passing flaneur. By using the shop window metaphor, Apple continues the rhetorical strategy featured in the "Think Different" ad, namely, to reanimate historically loaded cultural signifiers as a means of imagining the computer nostalgically and allegorically, thereby naturalizing and enchanting its presence.

The retro jazz soundtrack for the ad works as a nostalgic signifier.[28] This strategy is effective because it implicitly acknowledges two important facets of consumer technology culture. The use of familiar cultural symbols is comforting. Technology products are often perceived as being complicated and hard to use or figure out. Apple has also maintained an intuitive design strategy, making the experience of using a computer seem like something familiar that is just being recalled. This is an important strategy for technology marketers who seek to sell the future while trying not to evoke its associated anxieties. Early computer advertisements rarely showed the user.[29] The experience of using a computer was portrayed as a disembodied one, the mind of the user fusing with the computer to accomplish tasks. In the "Window" ad, however, the active presence of the user suggests the integration of the thinking self, the body, and the machine. This rhetorical move signifies computer and user as an integrated unit. The metaphor suggests that computers are not to be viewed as outside threats but as intimate and integrated extensions of our own human faculties. The man is looking at himself just as much as he is looking at the impish machine. This recalls the Greek Narcissus myth where the young man is transfixed by his own reflection in the pool of water but does not recognize the reflection as himself. The attraction of technology stems in part from our admiration of ourselves.[30]

Personal technology points us back to ourselves. The Narcissus myth is revived in the guise of the gawking consumer. The man sees the computer as a separate entity, and yet the computer responds to his every move as if he were looking in a mirror. The computer symbolizes an extension of human thought, communication, and memory. In the process of personification, the rhetoric of the Apple ads recalls the narcissism at the heart of the human-computer exchange. The allure of the computer screen is linked to an ability to fill it with things that mirror the self. From emails to photos to work documents, the window of the computer screen presents the user with extensions of his or her own creativity, productivity, sociability, and memory. The marrying of human and machine consciousness suggested by the "I think, therefore iMac" ad is repeated in the "Window" ad as the man comes to realize that his admiration for the machine is due in part to how well it mirrors himself.[31]

Marshall McLuhan would say that we are narcotized by these technological extensions of ourselves because they extend our own

34 abilities while at the same time inducing atrophy. Just as the motorcar paralyzes the action of the legs by effortlessly transporting the human body from one place to another, the computer externalizes memory, imagination, and communication. The iMac ad captures the relationship between humans and their tools in the metaphor of the mimetic dance between man and machine.

Ads and cultural texts are polysemous—meaning there is more than one valid interpretation. Another connotation evoked in the "Window" ad is the father looking in on a newborn child in the whitewashed hospital nursery. The familiar scene of the father peering into a nursery window to ogle his new offspring is playfully re-created in the iMac ad as the man smiles adoringly through the sanitized window at the steel, plastic, and glass extension of himself. The iMac can be read as progeny. The computer is more than an instrument for increasing productivity; it is an emotional and creative being capable of humor and empathy. At the introduction of the first Macintosh in 1984, Steve Jobs allowed the computer to "speak" using groundbreaking text to speech software. The fledgling Macintosh introduced Jobs by saying, "It is with considerable pride that I introduce a man who has been like a father to me, Steve Jobs."

The iMac "Window" ad is laden with evocative signifiers that mythologize the personal computer. The use of a nostalgic jazz tune coupled with the enchantment of the shop window reminds the viewer of a simpler time. Rather than being flooded with images, the iMac flaneur is arrested by the singular aura of the solitary iMac. He is able to contemplate the device and interact with it in an intimate way that reveals the spirit of the machine. The dualism of black and white, darkness and light, gives the advertising communication a metaphysical quality, and the lighthearted dance between man and machine personalizes the computer in a way that gives it a life of its own.[32]

"Get a Mac" ad campaign

36 The Mac Became Flesh

In May 2006 Apple launched the "Get a Mac" campaign. In the ads the Apple allegory of anthropomorphizing the machine reaches an apotheosis as the machines are no longer present but are instead portrayed by human actors. The ads ran on television until October 2009. There were sixty-six ads in the "Get a Mac" series, all directed by Phil Morrison of Epoch Films for TBWA Media Arts Lab. The setup of each ad is nearly identical. Actors John Hodgman and Justin Long stand side by side against a white background. Hodgman is typically dressed in a business suit. He wears glasses, and his hair is neatly combed to one side. Long is dressed casually, his shirt untucked and hair tousled. Long begins each ad by saying, "Hello, I'm a Mac," and Hodgman replies, "And I'm a PC." The two actors then engage in a humorous spoken-word exchange in which PC suffers from his own ineptitude. Mac remains somewhat aloof as he tries to convey sympathy to PC while also extolling the benefits of the Mac hardware and operating system. PC is reminded of his shortcomings, while Mac communicates the ways in which Mac computers transcend those shortcomings.

The "Get a Mac" ads are playful and humorous and tend to resist a deeper read (see p. 35). Their visual simplicity is inviting and helps reinforce one of Apple's persistent themes, that personal computing should not be intimidating. The PC character, played by John Hodgman, resembles a chubby Bill Gates and the comic strip character Dilbert, a hapless corporate functionary. Justin Long, who plays Mac, has been featured in a number of popular Hollywood films and television shows, making him well known to the young Macintosh demographic. The "Get a Mac" ads rely on a metaphor that equates the human actors with the hardware and software of their respective computer systems. The ads speak to the way in which technology has been personified but also to the ways in which humans have been technologized. As Marshall McLuhan put it, "We shape our tools and thereafter our tools shape us."[33]

In a January 2007 ad, PC appears dressed in a surgical gown. Mac asks if PC is going in for a checkup, and PC explains that he is going in to upgrade his operating system, "which is great, but I get a little nervous when they mess around with my insides." PC laments that they have to update his graphics card, memory, and processors: "it's major surgery." PC is visibly nervous and ends the commercial by saying, "Listen, Mac, if I don't come back, I want you to have my peripherals." The biological analogy between computer parts and the human body reminds us that the metaphors that guide computer development come from our own human faculties, particularly cognition and memory. The reverse is also true. Our sense of self is now shaped by the technologies that are used to diagnose and repair the body.[34] The humor of the Apple ads masks the deeper philosophical questions that arise when body and machine are imagined in such similar terms.

It is easy to assume that the two actors in the "Get a Mac" campaign represent PC and Mac users, but the intent is clearly to grant the operating systems a human personality. The way in which the actors are dressed, their body language, and their physical appearance are all signifiers to be transferred to the computer. The PC is dressed in a business suit. The Mac dresses more casually, often wearing T-shirts, jeans, sweatshirts, and the occasional untucked button-down shirt. Mac's hair is longer, and his upper lip and chin are sometimes unshaved. The Mac actor connotes being young and laid-back, eschewing the uptight world of the business person/machine. In an August 2006 spot called "Self Pity," Mac is dressed in a suit, and PC abruptly asks, "What's with the big boy clothes?" Mac replies that he was at a meeting and that he can run the same office software as PC. Here the Mac asserts his superiority by suggesting that he can do all the things PC can do when called upon. The PC is discouraged by this and curls up on the floor in a fetal position while moaning, "I'll just lie here and depreciate."

In addition to transferring various physical traits to the computer, the campaign also toys with the idea of computers having an emotional life. Two ads in the "Get a Mac" campaign feature a psychotherapist who tries to help PC overcome his deficiencies. In "Counselor" from October 2006, PC says he feels inadequate because he gets viruses and cannot do as much. Mac tries to reassure him, and the therapist asks Mac to say something positive about PC: "OK, easy. PC you are a wizard with numbers and you dress like a gentleman." PC responds by saying that he guesses Mac is better with "creative stuff," even though it is "juvenile and a waste of time." In the "Breakthrough" ad from April 2008, the therapist assures PC that his issues are not his fault. She reasons that PC's components come from all over while Mac's all come from the same place, so how could PC possibly work well? PC's realization that it is not his fault seems to be a breakthrough until he utters the punch line, "It's not my fault . . . it's Mac's fault," after which they all sit down again to continue the session.

The female therapist is a reminder that the gender of Mac and PC is also an important signifier in the ad. Females appear very infrequently throughout the campaign. The therapist appears in two ads, and she seems to connote the idea that females are better working with emotional issues. In another ad from April 2008, a female yoga instructor works with PC to help him forget the many problems of his Vista operating system. As she recites the things he should be putting out of his mind, she reminds herself that her yoga studio billing was "screwed up" by Vista and storms off the set, to which the PC quips, "Maybe I should try Pilates." Here a female represents another empathic figure, but in this case she cannot control her own emotions.[35]

Several other ads feature females who are seeking a new computer. The male-female dynamic of the Mac/PC and the interested female consumer sets up a "courtship" scenario where the two machines vie for the woman's affection/purchase by showcasing their relative merits. In the August 2009 "Top of the Line" ad, PC introduces a young woman to a top-of-the-line PC played by an actor dressed in a dark suit who conveys a comic smugness. The woman says that she wants a big screen and a fast processor. The top-of-the-line PC says "look no further" and "some say I'm too fast." The dating metaphor seems an apt one for the consumer-product relationship.

In an interview with MIT psychologist Sherry Turkle in 1982, a woman in her early thirties said, "I'm programmed to fall for the same kind of man every time. I'm like a damned computer stuck in a loop. . . . I guess my cards are punched out the same way."[36] However, the same woman was careful not to conflate the computer metaphor with her emotional life, "When people fall in love . . . it's like a blinding emotion. Computers don't have anything to do with that."[37] Apple's imaginative coup was to dissolve the dichotomy between the processing mind and the emotional mind. The Apple computer is positioned as a smart and emotional machine.

The "Get a Mac" ads present a tension that Apple has nurtured for the past thirty years. Windows/PC computers represent the world of work and the depersonalization wrought by technology, while Apple computers are part of a creative and romanticized movement to liberate human creativity. This motif is evident in the "1984" ad that ushered in the personal computer age and persists in humorous form in the "Get a Mac" campaign. Like a medieval morality play that dramatized man's plight as a fall from innocence followed by redemption, the PC represents the "fall" of technology while Mac provides the necessary redemption.

The "Get a Mac" ads create a dualism between the worlds of work and leisure. From a philosophical perspective, work and creativity are bound up with the ways in which culture is understood. According to Josef Pieper, "[C]ulture depends for its very existence on leisure, and leisure, in its turn, is not possible unless it has a durable and consequently living link with the cultus, with divine worship."[38] Leisure, for Pieper, is the ultimate act of freedom in which the human being is permitted the time and space for contemplation. In the world of total work, where reaction time trumps contemplation, our intellectual, moral, and spiritual senses can atrophy.

Apple promotes a return to leisure. It is a radical proposition that takes the ultimate symbol of work in the information age, the personal computer, and reimagines it as a mode of escape from the drudgery of work. From the Dionysian feasts of the Greeks to the feast days of

40 the Catholic liturgical calendar, religious ritual has historically provided the foundation for the nourishment and rejuvenation of humans "born to work in painful toil."[39] The "Get a Mac" actors play allegorical roles, acting out the conflict between the human spirit of creativity and the dreary environment of labor and soulless efficiency in thirty-second vignettes. Leisure has traditionally been for escaping the everyday and taking time to make sense of the world. Historically this has meant that leisure has been occupied with contemplation and worship. In the modern age, however, the ethics of speed, productivity, and efficiency have transformed leisure activities. The computer and other media devices have become supreme leisure objects, things to fill the silence between the activities of the day.

 The Apple allegory begins with an inverted creation account where the woman in the "1984" ad releases the divine light of Macintosh to enlighten humanity through an act of radical disobedience. The heroine bears the half-eaten Apple logo on her chest as a badge of honor for her disobedience and willingness to challenge the IBM status quo. The mythical framework introduced in "1984" is maintained more than a decade later in the "Think Different" campaign in which the company's countercultural values are embodied in a nostalgic parade of countercultural visionaries who rejected standard conventions. A persistent theme in the Macintosh ads is personification of computers by granting them emotion and personality. The morality plays of the "Get a Mac" campaign position Apple computers as objects of leisure, diametrically opposed to the soulless world of work and corporate conformity. The irony is that Macintosh devotees constitute their own culture of conformity, pledging fealty to the Apple brand.

2

iPod Devotion

Acoustic Ecstasy and Altered States

n October 2001, Steve Jobs unveiled Apple's portable digital music player, iPod, to a relatively sedate group of journalists and investors. The announcement was not typical for an Apple product launch. The public mood was somber after the terrorist attacks of 9/11, just three weeks prior. Absent were the cheering throngs of Apple devotees and the religious revival atmosphere. The subdued iPod introduction belied its enormous cultural impact, however. Apple has sold more than a quarter billion iPods worldwide.[1] In 2004 *Newsweek* christened millions of iPod users "iPod Nation" and announced that the music player had gone from gizmo to "life-changing cultural icon."[2] iTunes, the software for downloading iPod content, has surpassed sixteen billion downloaded songs.[3] The market for add-ons is a billion-dollar business and growing. iPod accessories include armbands, speakers, clock radios, cases, and plug-ins that track exercise and biorhythms. iPods are workout companions, fashion accessories, portable DJs, and tokens of membership in the Apple technology cult.

For many iPod users, the device has acquired sacred status. The iPod has been called an "object of devotion" that has inspired a "cult of iPod."[4] iPod owners comment on the device's ability to make them feel "cosmically connected"[5] to their music and to make their surroundings seem more "spiritual and sacred."[6] iPod users describe the experience of transcending the here and now by being physically present but mentally elsewhere.[7] One iPod fan reports, "High as a kite off the exercise, the music transports me to nirvana. Sometimes, when the right tune pops up, I'm truly in heaven."[8] Others describe the iPod as a mood regulator and a "contemplative device."[9]

The religious metaphors favored by iPod enthusiasts are not unique to iPod; instead, they represent the abiding relationship between aesthetic experience and religious feeling. The German philosopher Friedrich Schleiermacher believed that music was the art form best suited for expressing religious feeling.[10] Thomas Carlyle noted, "Music is well said to be the speech of angels."[11] And British essayist Walter Pater declared, "[A]ll art constantly aspires to the condition of music."[12] For Pater, music is the highest form of art because it appeals to our "imaginative reason." Poetry, painting, and music all leave impressions that reach beyond sense and intellect to stir the soul. The impressions left by music are largely incommunicable. The iPod's religious resonance stems in part from the elusive quality of musical union, the aesthetic pleasure wherein sense and intellect are saturated with the unutterable feelings cultivated by music.

The challenge for Apple's iPod advertising team would be communicating the largely incommunicable experience of musical immersion. When TBWA/Chiat/Day art director Susan Alinsangan and writer Tom Kraemer were tasked with creating a small billboard campaign for the new iPod, they had little clue that their compaign would become one of the most iconic in Apple history.[13] The standard Apple formula for new product ads was sharp product photography on a gleaming, white background. The visual effect is clean, elegant, and pure. The agency creative team wanted to take iPod in a different direction though. The creative team developed a concept that featured silhouettes of individual dancers set on a neon background. A pair of white wires streamed from a white handheld device into the ears of the gyrating actors. Apple's lead product designer, Jony Ive, felt like the white wires and earphones connoted purity.[14] It would be the only instance of white featured in the new look advertising.

When the concepts were presented to Steve Jobs, the creative team all stood at one end of the table hoping Jobs would gravitate to the silhouette designs. Jobs did not like the look of the ads at first. He felt as though they were off-brand and not Apple.[15] He wanted the sparkling product shots. Yet the creative team made a hard sell. An outspoken Brit on the team, James Vincent, who joined the agency to help TBWA connect with the millennial generation, played up the fact that the visuals embodied the intensely emotional and personal experience users have with their music.[16] Jobs eventually bought in and, like all savvy CEOs, took credit for making the decision to pull the trigger on the iconic campaign.

The billboard campaign ran in trendy urban centers like Paris, Berlin, New York, Amsterdam, Los Angeles, and Montreal. The towering spectacles were stark departures, not just for Apple, but also for outdoor advertising in general. More than just another crass canvas of consumerism, the iPod ads looked like installation art (see p. 44). They were the stained glass windows of the urban cathedral. Rather than commemorating saints, the images celebrated the radical individuality that comes with controlling one's own sonic universe. The ads work mythically by summoning an image of ecstatic experience, bathing it in preternatural light, and casting iPod in the role of sacramental object.

The iconic function of the iPod ads recalls the religious metaphors invoked by iPod enthusiasts—the iPod as "object of devotion" and "contemplative device." The iPod is a totemic object, one that connects the user to the intangible pleasures of music and a broader community of consumers. The work of advertising is to reinforce this totemism by providing the visual symbols and structures of meaning by which these sensual and communal connections are made.[17] In this way, advertising functions like religious communication. The structures of meaning traditionally provided by art and religion have been absorbed into capitalist consumption and imagery.[18]

iPod ad campaign

The iPod ads can thus be read as techno-religious icons. Religious
communication tends to exhibit three rhetorical features: the use of
metaphor, the presence of symbols that cannot be reduced to nonfigu-
rative forms of expression, and an allusion to metaphysical concepts.[19]
In the iPod ads, the dancing silhouettes are visual metaphors for the
euphoria brought on by musical immersion. The emotional and spiritual experiences described by iPod users resist reduction to nonfigura-
tive forms of expression. The silhouetted symbols used to connote the
pleasures of aural immersion are opaque because the sensation cannot
be reduced to literal terms. They are instances of symbolical realism—
a rhetorical attempt to describe an experience that eludes description.
Emotional reactions to music are hard to put into words. Scholars of
rhetoric have noted the way in which symbolical realism allows for
the portrayal of an iconic hypostasis or a "concrete representation
of a spiritual quality."[20] The iPod ads dabble in the metaphysical by
attempting to portray a peak metaphysical experience in irreducible
metaphorical terms.

Dancing in the Dark

The first televised silhouette spot for iPod in 2003 featured an up-
and-coming band called The Black Eyed Peas. The song featured
was "Hey Mama," a genre-bending song blending hip-hop, reggae,
and tribal percussion. The "Hey Mama" ad was part of a trio of 2003
iPod television ads that featured silhouettes dancing on colored backgrounds. The ads are striking in their simplicity. Their minimalism is
consistent with the aesthetic of Apple machines, lacking ornamenta-
tion and stripped down to essential forms. In the ads, silhouettes of
human figures dance energetically while connected to white iPods via
the signature white wires and earbuds. The background of the scene
is a rotating series of neon colors. In the spots, individual dancers are
featured in rapid succession, creating a kaleidoscopic effect of kinetic
energy and color. The ghostly figures dance to the beat of music in an
ebullient display of rhythmic movement.

46   The figure of the silhouette serves an important rhetorical function in the way in which the ads and the product are imagined. In one view, the lack of dimensionality resists a "deeper" read. Two-dimensional figures dancing on horizonless backgrounds appear to be no more than animated shadows just enjoying the music. If we read "lack of dimension" as a signifier, we may consider the steamrolling of identity brought on by the advent of screen-based technology. Life online is characterized by two-dimensional representations of the self. Avatars, emoticons, text, and photographs serve as signifiers of personality and emotion in the absence of body language, inflection, and physical presence. This symptom of life in digital culture is also represented by the silhouette campaign. As such, the iPod and the experience of auditory immersion and dance serve as a mode of resistance to the flattening of identity. Dance is an expression of the entire body. It is kinetic and physical, both qualities that run counter to the sedentary posture attributed to computer use. The paradoxical allure of Apple iconography is its ability to identify the social tensions brought on by greater technology use while also offering redemption from its more pessimistic consequences.

    The shadow dancers also connote a dualism of presence and absence. This reflects the iPod experience in which users are physically present but mentally elsewhere as they listen to music. They exhibit an "absent presence."[21] In a reversal of contemporary image advertising where actors are chosen for their ability to be seen, the iPod actors are opaque and anonymous. The metaphor of anonymity can be extended to the act of iPod listening itself—a practice that discourages the type of personal interaction that leads to familiarity.

    While the lyrics are important signifiers for interpreting the meaning of the ad, the beat of the music provides another important layer of meaning. Like most modern music, the song does not fit cleanly in a single musical genre. The iPod campaign samples artists from multiple musical genres to appeal to listeners who prefer different types of music. "Hey Mama" by The Black Eyed Peas is a combination of hip-hop, dance, and reggae. In the context of American popular music and culture, the reggae sound was co-opted by a number of different artists, particularly dance artists who favor the distinctive beat and African rhythms. As a form of social expression, African dance loses some of its political weight when it is mass produced for dance halls. At the same time, it illustrates a social tension between music for relaxation and music as site of spiritual tension. The tension of reggae music was tailor-made for the ritual space of the dance hall, where physical exertion also becomes a symbol for liberation from oppression.[22]

The rise of the iPod is tied to the rise of the DJs who modified dance hall culture in the 1990s. In *The Cult of iPod* Leander Kahney describes the ways in which iPod DJ parties factored into the cultural adoption of the technological form. Because of its similarity to the sound system DJs who "liberated" black music from the black community, the iPod permitted a blending of sounds and genres by virtue of its capacious storage capacity.[23] The tribal reggae beat of the "Hey Mama" ad along with the black silhouettes hail the viewer as black.[24] The ad is an invitation to participate in the liberating dance-hall experience of the black community through the iPod. The "Hey Mama" ad demonstrates that the spiritual resonance of the iPod ad is not limited to the metaphysical connotations of dancing shadows. The religious resonance of the iPod also works at the social and political levels, where narratives of liberation are embedded in the musical genres presented in the campaign.

Till We Have Faces

Masks are an ancient means of surrendering one's own identity and assuming a new extraordinary identity.[25] The iPod silhouette signifies the idea of being masked, concealing the identity of the listener. The mask as a cultural form has been layered with a number of diverse meanings and associations. With the exception of the Arabic world, where Islamic belief has prohibited deification of characters, the mask is a common artifact among a variety of religious traditions. Ritual masks are most commonly used to depict spiritual mythologies

48 in material form.[26] In the Buddhist tradition of the Himalayas, animal spirits battle demonic forces and protect followers from natural calamities. In ancient Greece, masks of animals and the grotesque were infused with animistic spirits and were used in ritual processions and dances. The masks were also offered as votive gifts to the gods, sometimes even becoming cult idols themselves.[27]

The mask as signifier in the iPod silhouette ads acquired additional meaning with the launch of a series of ads featuring the faces of well-known recording artists. Like the other silhouette ads in the campaign, it is the music that animates the October 2004 ad for "iPod + iTunes." However, this is the first time that we see the artist performing the song. In this case it is the band U2 performing the song "Vertigo." This is a subtle but significant departure from the formula of the other iPod silhouette ads. In previous print and television ads, the identity of the dancers had always been obscured by the absence of a face. Now, the faces of the commercial figures are visible. Their bodies remain black, but their faces reflect a soft spotlight that matches the hue of the background. The band's instruments and microphones are plugged in via the signature white wire.

The "Viva la Vida" iPod ad features the British band Coldplay and opens with a silhouetted Chris Martin, the lead singer of the band. As the music builds, the black background is illuminated by a burst of purple fog as Martin sings, "I used to rule the world." Martin seems to influence the dispersion of the illuminated fog with the motion of his hand. A number of lens flares and orbs of light seem to issue forth from the rising fog resembling a cosmic supernova. The blending of rock and symphony in the song lends itself to the dance of light and fog being conducted by the rhythmic movement of the band members. Lighted trails follow the head of the guitar as it moves with the music. The camera returns to Martin and pulls back as his raised hand seems to attract the rising fog and lighted orbs behind him. The singer continues, "Seas would rise when I gave the word." The lyrics of the refrain include, "I hear Jerusalem bells ringing, / Roman Calvary choirs are singing, / Be my mirror, my sword, my shield, / My missionaries in a foreign field."

The musical artists are demigods in the iPod mythology. U2, Coldplay, and the other artists featured in the campaign are manufacturers of the muse that induces the fits of ecstasy and passion that private iPod listening provides. As such, they are given faces. They are more present than the anonymous listeners who faithfully download the music. The silhouette is a reflection of the consumer's absent presence while wearing the iPod. By donning the white earbuds and channeling the musical gods, the iPod listener takes part in a mobile, private, and anonymous ritual practice that has become nearly universal in digital culture.

Re-enchanting the City

The rise of iPod culture is the latest example of the perennial symbiosis between the stuff of culture and the technologies that shape that culture. In the information society, we have entered a peculiar recursive loop: popular mythologies about technology are being amplified and circulated by the very same technology that is being mythologized. In the industrial age, the "myth of the machine"[28] referred to the social transformation wrought by mass production and automation. While citizens of the industrial era developed notions of self-identity from the agricultural or urban machine environments in which they were situated, their experience was far different from that of the citizens of the media technology age. In the current environment, myths of progress and technological achievement are proffered, processed, and promulgated by the very inventions and tools that are being imagined mythically, media technology.

An iPod ad called "Cubicle" expresses this dynamic in visual form. The "Cubicle" ad for the iPod nano 1G begins with a shot of a single album cover set against a black background. The album cover, Beck's *Guero*, quickly unfolds into a series of album covers from other artists, including The Doors, Van Halen, and The Black Eyed Peas. The album covers remain interconnected as they continue to expand and take the form of skyscrapers and buildings in a virtual cityscape.

50 The camera circles the animated scene as the albums unfold in ever-expanding three-dimensional patterns. The effect is dizzying. The city is massive, but it looks like a house of cards ready to fall at any moment. At the pivotal moment in the ad, all of the structures begin to collapse. All of the album art is sucked into a vortex. As the camera tilts down, we see the albums being sucked into an iPod nano in a torrential spiral flow. The image invokes the media torrent described by critic Todd Gitlin, "[Media] is everywhere, too much to take in. It is, in a sense, like nature—that overwhelming presence human beings once found so threatening yet auspicious that they conjured gods and demons to imagine their way through its ungraspable allness."[29]

We know by the shape of the structures that the assembly of albums is supposed to represent a city, but it is a hastily constructed metropolis, one liable to fall at any moment. When the inevitable collapse occurs, the lyricist begins to wail in a primal scream. It is here that two distinct metaphors take shape. One metaphor is the death of the album brought on by the iPod. With individual songs available for download for ninety-nine cents, the era of the fifteen-dollar album has passed. This benefits manufactured pop artists like Britney Spears and American Idol winners but alienates more conceptual groups like Wilco, Radiohead, and Pink Floyd. So, on one level we are presented with a visual metaphor for the end of the album era as the tracks disintegrate into a grouping of songs that draw from thousands of different albums, none of which have to be purchased in full.

At a deeper level, the album metropolis works metaphorically as a symbol for the immateriality of digital media. Digital music is drained of the materiality of analog media, a form remembered for lush album art, LPs, and cassettes. The matter and form were once separated, so that one could develop an attachment to a song and to the particular record on which it was stored. It was a relationship that lent itself to fetishism. The fetish object is now the iPod—a universal container for the thousands of individual fetish objects that have abandoned their material embodiment in tangible media to join the ephemeral realm of digitized data. The signifier of the musical city is absorbed into the all-encompassing iPod. It is a depiction worthy of Buddhist philosophy in which the enlightened soul is freed from the evils of material existence by being annihilated and absorbed into a unity of divine oneness.

The third connotation recalls the circumstances of the iPod's launch, a month after the 9/11 terrorist attacks in the United States when jet airplanes smashed into skyscrapers and leveled a section of lower Manhattan. The era of televisual terrorism provided a global witness to the destruction of that day, and the psychic damage was as profound in San Francisco as it was in New York City. Society was in need of a mediated antidote.

Following the shock, there was something needed to fill the void and address the psychological damage that had been done. In 1900 sociologist Georg Simmel described urban culture in a way that presaged the utility of the iPod:

> The jostling crowdedness and the motley disorder of metro-
> politan communication . . . would . . . be unbearable with-
> out . . . psychological distance. Since contemporary urban
> culture . . . forces us to be physically close to an enormous
> number of people, . . . people would sink completely into
> despair if the objectification of social relationships did not
> bring with it an inner boundary and reserve. The pecuniary
> character of relationships, either openly or concealed in a
> thousand forms, places [a] . . . functional distance between
> people that is an inner protection . . . against the overcrowded
> proximity.[30]

Simmel's critique is referring to the economic character of relation-ships in the modern city. On a normal day, occupations define social identities and serve as a psychological barrier between thousands of anonymous individuals. In the jarring moment of apocalyptic destruction the social boundaries are dissolved. The city's monads become communal. Functional distinctions are momentarily forgot-ten as everyone becomes subject to the catastrophic spectacle. An

52   ad hoc religion emerges in which everyone prays for deliverance from the unbearable circumstances. But the moment is fleeting, and something else is ultimately needed to numb the pain. Those who embrace urban life are accustomed to surprise and instability—it is part of what makes city life so stimulating. However, after 9/11 and the incessant replay of the event, the impulse was to change the channel. With the iPod, urban dwellers found a way to move through the tumult of the decapitated city by numbing the pain and self-medicating with music.

The iPod tableau ultimately presents us with an allegory about media environments. Cities are composed of concrete, steel, and glass monuments that kindle the anxieties of early-twentieth-century agrarians who detest urbanization for its atomizing tendencies. On the other hand, the urban environment is exhilarating. The iPod "Cubicle" ad is emblematic of the city and its tensions as it reconfigures our sensory environment. The city, represented by the towers of album art, is no longer something to be experienced out there, but in the mind. Charles Baudelaire wrote about the city, "The giddiness felt in great cities is analogous to that felt in the midst of nature. . . . Religious intoxication of big cities. Pantheism. I am all; all are me."[31]

The iPod "Wild Postings" ad ran from May to October 2004. Unlike the previous ads that are set in an abstract space, "Wild Postings" is set in the physicality of an urban environment. The ad does not open with a musical soundtrack; instead, the soundtrack is the city street, car engines, and police sirens. A man walks the streets of the city plugged into his iPod. The scenes recall the flaneur who soaks in all the sensory stimulation of the city.[32] Now, the traveler is removed, detached, engaged in a species of "angelism," wherein discarnate music and voices flood the ear, blocking the embodied sounds of the city that once enchanted the urban drifter. The actor encounters a pedestrian walking several dogs and another with a child on his shoulders. The association is that the iPod is a technological form of companionship. If the leashes mirror the wires of the iPod, then the child on the man's shoulders represents the earphones, the child's legs providing an affectionate embrace around the ears. The scene is a visual metaphor for the companionship that the iPod offers.

The iPod user passes a row of handbills or "wild postings" that cover the wall next to the sidewalk. The posters comprise twenty-six iPod silhouette ads. Here, the most recognizable signifier of the iPod campaign, the dancing silhouette, becomes part of another iPod ad. Here, Apple engages in the rhetorical act of parodic self-reference. The mosaic of posters provides the only color in the frame. The buildings, the wall, and even a leafless tree in front of the wall are rendered lifeless next to the kinetic and colorful posters. Rhetorically, the ad showcases the "centricity" of the iPod experience.[33] The actions of the dancers emanate from the "generating core of the self." The concept is distinguished from eccentricity in which individuals interact with other "centers" in the social field. Centricity is ultimately an insular experience in which none of the individuals make contact with other individuals. They are isolated yet homogenized. Their eccentricities remain private and personal choices in music.

The shot composition features a tree in the foreground striking a pose that seems to mimic the dancers, its arms pushing outward and reaching for the transcendent high that the music delivers. In a subtle symbolic reversal, it is the ads that are imbued with an animistic spirit while the tree remains lifeless. The "mother tree" of Germanic pagan lore looks rather stodgy standing in front of the posters, her branches awkwardly outstretched in an attempt to mimic the contorted bliss of ecstatic dance. This telling contrast shows the way in which the "nature" of city life is not found in the biological remnants that stubbornly share the ground with the concrete. Rather, the "nature" of city life is reflected in its native advertising and technology.

The ads are the most visually arresting element in the scene and also the most enchanted. The figures on the poster dance to the music of the actor's iPod as he walks by, pausing only when he pauses the song on his iPod to take in this strange occurrence. It is this encounter with the animated spirits of the iPod images that ultimately stops the actor in his tracks. Neither the marvels of modern architecture that surround him nor the multitude of other real human beings that cross his path seem worthy of a second glance. The actor traverses the city wrapped in a sonorous envelope, glibly acknowledging the other human beings as passing shadows on his acoustic pleasure cruise. Only when the actor is confronted with the dancing shadows of the ads come-to-life is he jolted from his narcotized state. He must stop the music to confirm that he indeed has the power to animate these paper spirits. When the music stops, they stop dancing. When the music resumes, they resume dancing. Their response is a metaphor for what the iPod listener experiences in this particular form of "mobile privatization," that his or her surroundings are heavily mediated and therefore entirely programmable.

Altered States

iPod advertising celebrates the ways in which the device stimulates mood and alters the listener's sensory relationship to the surrounding environment. According to Steve Jobs, one of his most formative experiences involved listening to music in an altered state. In Jobs' first experience on LSD, the shaman of high tech recalled something that sounds like the treatment for an iPod commercial: "All of a sudden the wheat field was playing Bach. It was the most wonderful experience of my life up to that point. I felt like the conductor of this symphony with Bach coming through the wheat field."[34]

Jobs was part of a group of counterculturalists in the 1960s who identified as wireheads—a group of hippies who also loved electronics. Jobs subscribed to the idea that computers could be a tool, like drugs, for elevating consciousness. The analogy was not lost on counterculture guru Timothy Leary, whose well-publicized experiments with LSD are good examples of a persistent desire to fiddle with consciousness for the purpose of seeking spiritual enlightenment. Leary championed the use of LSD as a way to expand human consciousness and drop out of the "tribal game."[35] Leary's social movement utilized and embraced all manner of religious metaphor to further the cause.

In 1966 Leary founded the League for Spiritual Discovery, a religion declaring LSD as its holy sacrament. Thirty years later, Leary called the personal computer the "LSD of the 1990s":

> It's well known that most of the creative impulse in the software industry, and indeed much of the hardware, particularly at Apple Macintosh, derived directly from the sixties consciousness movement. [The Apple cofounder] Steve Jobs went to India, took a lot of acid, studied Buddhism, and came back and said that Edison did more to influence the human race than the Buddha. And [Microsoft founder Bill] Gates was a big psychedelic person at Harvard. It makes perfect sense to me that if you activate your brain with psychedelic drugs, the only way you can describe it is electronically.[36]

Steve Jobs' LSD experience in the wheat field reinforces the idea that drugs and computers have a history of being imagined as gateways to altered consciousness.

The iPod gives new meaning to the term "wirehead"—as countless Apple disciples now walk around with wires hanging from their heads. Some of the iPod advertising playfully references the analogous relationship between mind-altering pharmacology and technology. The iPod nano 2G "Listen to the Music" silhouette ad features dancers holding glowing iPods that leave trails on the dark background. The only light in the scene comes from the device itself. The iPods in each scene are held in the hand rather than attached to the body, and they glow with vibrant greens, pinks, and blues. The music is hypnotic, the refrain "Listen, listen to the music" is repeated in a cult-like chant. The artist Cut Chemist creates acid house music, a genre known for repetitive beats with spoken-word refrains, designed to induce a state of trance.

The sweeping movements of the iPod dancers paint the air with neon light emanating from the iPod. A trail follows each of their movements in an apparent reference to the effect of seeing trails when high on acid. One is also reminded of the use of glow sticks at rave events. An anonymous twenty-one-year-old female describes the rave experience this way: "Sometimes when I walk into a rave and smell the familiar scent of incense, the sight of glow sticks, and the overpowering beat of trance, I get this light-headed sensation and sense of weightlessness in my body that reminds me of the first experience I had on E. It's awesome."[37]

The rave experience has a mystical intensity for its participants, who enjoy an altered state of consciousness among the musical, technological, and chemical delights. The iPod ad suggests that the rave experience has also been made mobile and personal. The iPod is a narcotic that has domesticated and legalized the drug trip. Just as the rave offers participants a sensory overload that brings on ecstatic states of mind, the iPod promises a similar experience.

In an example of life imitating art, a phenomenon known as the silent rave has developed around the iPod's popularity. A silent rave is an event where participants gather in a predetermined location to listen to the same iPod playlist. The use of headphones precludes outside observers from hearing what the group is listening to, but the ravers remain in sync musically through their iPods. In April 2010, Harvard students collaborated with the American Repertory Theater to host a "Silent LED Rave." The event was dubbed an "art and social experiment" that was designed to "visualize music."[38] Students downloaded a playlist beforehand that also contained a special LED color that would light up the device screen when the music was played. The notion that one can visualize the aesthetic high of music lies at the heart of the iPod campaign.

The ecstatic inducements that fill the iPod advertising narrative beg a note of warning from philosopher of technology Jacques Ellul:

> We must conclude that it is far from accidental that ecstatic phenomena have developed to the greatest degree in the most technicized societies. And it is to be expected that these phenomena will continue to increase. This indicates nothing less

than the subjection of mankind's new religious life to technique. . . . Ecstasy is subject to the world of technique and its servant.[39]

The ecstatic experience once reserved for religious rapture and eros has taken up residence in the technologically mediated experiences of musical immersion and the pleasures of the modern city. There is no zero-sum game between secularism and religion wherein the two worldviews are locked in an eternal struggle to the death. Instead, the popular technologies and their iconic representations that fill the cultural landscape invoke the archetypal symbols and mystical impulses poached from the misty realms of religion. In this rhetorical cross-breeding, "the cult of iPod" becomes a metonym for the ways in which technology and transcendence remain joined at the hip and plugged into our ears.

3

iPhone Worship
"Touching is believing"

Steve Jobs' first experience designing telephones involves the now famous story of the "blue box" device. In the early 1970s, Jobs' friend Steve Wozniak was captivated by an *Esquire* story about the creator of a phone-hacking device that made it possible to dial long distance calls for free.[1] Wozniak got to work on his own version of the device right away using his own components. Jobs and Wozniak invited John Draper, aka "Captain Crunch," one of the mysterious men featured in the *Esquire* article, to Wozniak's Berkeley dormitory to show them how to make the box work. Draper was hesitant but ultimately acquiesced. By the end of the evening, the three intrepid hackers decided that their first call should be to the Vatican. It worked.

The Pope and the "Jesus Phone"

Thirty-five years later, Jobs would introduce the iPhone—a device that would transform the wireless telephone industry. The hacker-turned-billionaire Steve Jobs inadvertently found his prized new device linked to the Vatican again. The iPhone became the subject of a host of religious parodies, most notably earning the moniker "Jesus phone." The godly description of Apple's signature gadget started with a joke by *Gizmodo* contributor Brian Lam. Lam coined the term "Jesus phone" in a blog post, and it quickly spread through the online tech news community.[2] The "Jesus phone" quip was posted in response to an address given by Pope Benedict XVI on Christmas morning in 2006. The Holy Father asked,

> Is a Saviour needed by a humanity which has invented interactive communication, which navigates in the virtual ocean of the internet and, thanks to the most advanced modern communications technologies, has now made the Earth, our great common home, a global village? This humanity of the twenty-first century appears as a sure and self-sufficient master of its own destiny, the avid proponent of uncontested triumphs.[3]

Benedict XVI's comments reveal one of the fundamental tensions of the modern religion-technology relationship: transcendent redemption has been part of mythology and religion for centuries, but the source of that redemption has relocated to the scientific and technological.[4] The Holy Father's concern stems from humanity's failure to provide for the basic material needs of hungry millions while millions of others engage in "unbridled consumerism." Lam responds,

> Of course we still need a Savior. Hopefully, our shepherd, Steve Jobs, will unveil Apple-Cellphone-Thingy, the true Jesus Phone—or jPhone—in two weeks, at the Macworld Keynote. It shall lift the hunger and disease you speak of from the land, as it will cure the rabid state of mind infecting Mac fanboys like yours truly.[5]

Lam responds to the pope's genuine appeal for reflection by co-opting the language of Christianity to describe his anticipation of technology in messianic terms. Here, Lam is engaging in the rhetorical act of "parodic allusion"—an intertextual strategy that appears throughout the divinized iPhone rhetoric.[6]

Lam's reflexive parody of the name Jesus is a hallmark of postmodernism. Since the advent of electronic media, the mass reproduction of messages and images has so exhausted meaningful cultural symbols that their recirculation now favors parody and ironic reference.[7] Devices like the iPhone that become the tools by which the recirculation of cultural symbols takes place amplify this rhetorical situation.[8] Text and images are manipulated, emailed, and messaged on the order of billions per day. Symbols and images often become Internet "memes" and go viral, making them part of the cultural lexicon overnight, "Jesus phone" being a case in point. The iPhone's central role in the production/reproduction and circulation/recirculation of symbols grants it an elevated status worthy of sublime descriptors like "Jesus phone." It is the symbol by which other cultural symbols are funneled and spread.

Technologies like the iPhone put us in touch with an immense, global, and decentered network. The scale of this network is only dimly perceivable.[9] It evokes sublime descriptors like "Jesus phone" because it alludes to something that cannot be shown or presented—where the imagination fails to produce an object to match the concept.[10] It works as both a promotional strategy (concealing the object before a highly anticipated launch) and philosophically by referring to the way in which immense telecommunications networks and the devices that harness them exceed our ability to explain their inner workings. The tendency is to fill in the blanks with terms and phrases that signify an excess of meaning or mystery.

Apple's flair for sublime design reached a high point in 2007 with the release of the iPhone. The iPhone combines telephone, Internet browsing, email, and scores of other web applications or "apps" on a powerful pocket computer. The web functionality of iMac and the mobility of iPod converged in the iPhone, making it a must-have device. The iPhone is revered for its elegance and simplicity. The device is operated almost exclusively by touchscreen gestures. It is a shimmering block of glass and textured metal that set the standard for smartphone design. Advertising for the iPhone was relatively sparse before the initial launch. The device was shrouded in secrecy, making the launch at the Macworld Conference in January 2007 borderline liturgical. Jobs told the audience at Macworld that the iPhone would "reinvent" the telecommunications sector, that it would "change everything," and that he felt very fortunate to work on just one product like this in his career. The holy trinity of telephone, iPod, and Internet would ensure that millions of iPhone customers would never feel disconnected again.

The sublime used to refer to the overwhelming sensation of recognizing the divine in the wonders of nature: oceans, mountains, and stars. Poets and painters would try to capture the natural sublime in verse and on canvas, but it was an elusive experience. When it was shared by many, it provided a collective sense of awe and unity, giving some confirmation that God's presence was something that could be experienced universally and in communion with others. The dawn of the industrial revolution shifted the center of collective wonder to the creative machines that made up the late-nineteenth-century landscape. Enormous factories, powerful machines, immense buildings and bridges humbled man in new and startling ways. An army of human creators fashioning a new Tower of Babel, a new nature, was outshining the Creator.[11]

A new nature requires a new set of myths for coming to grips with the new environment. The myth provides a narrative means of grappling with powers that seem beyond our individual control. It also "reinvests the landscape and the works of men with transcendent significance."[12] For the ancients, myths helped explain the capriciousness of nature. Weather and natural disaster were concrete signs from the gods that expressed divine favor or disappointment. Threats of blackout, crashes, and crippling computer viruses are among the fears of technological man.[13] The unsuspecting iPhone user who suddenly loses service in a dead zone or loses all of his or her contacts or, worse, loses the phone altogether enters a state of panic. This is a perfectly natural

iPhone "Touching is believing" ad campaign

64 reaction to the new environment in which we are situated. Being cut off from the communication infrastructure renders one deaf, dumb, and blind in a world dependent on 24/7 connection. The messianic tone of much of the iPhone hype then stems in part from its ability to heal and deliver the technologically disabled from the state of digital darkness.

The idolatry reserved for Apple products stems from its role as privileged cultural mediator, a symptom of which is the popular rhetoric ascribing it with sublime properties. The intertextual allusion and parody present in the technology journalism surrounding the iPhone launch are also present in the company's advertising. The lone print advertisement that preceded the launch of the iPhone was suggestive of this pattern. The ad features the tagline "Touching is believing" (see p. 63). The scene features an illuminated iPhone projecting its light into the surrounding darkness as a finger reaches in to make physical contact with the device. The visual effect of electronic light piercing the darkness plays a central role in the symbolic construction of the ad. The ad highlights the touchscreen technology that centers the user interface on the screen itself rather than a physical keypad. The Apple smartphone redefines not only the type of content that can be experienced on a mobile device but also the sensory means by which that content is accessed and experienced.

The phrase "Touching is believing" evokes the biblical account of the apostle Thomas, who refused to believe Christ had risen from the dead until he could touch the wounds of Jesus' crucifixion.[14] The seventeenth-century painting by Caravaggio depicting the doubting apostle Thomas placing his finger in Christ's wounded side is a graphical representation of the story from Scripture. According to John's gospel account, Thomas insisted that his belief in the risen Christ was contingent on touching the actual wounds: "Except I shall see in his hands the print of the nails and put my finger into the place of the nails and put my hand into his side, I will not believe" (John 20:25). Eight days later Christ would appear to Thomas and invite him to touch: "Put in thy finger hither and see my hands. And bring hither the hand and put it into my side. And be not faithless but believing" (John 20:27). The drama of the gospel account is parodied in the ad for iPhone and presented as an answer to the prayers of Apple fans anxious to see the new creation. In its unique positioning as a device driven almost exclusively by touchscreen commands, the linguistic signifier, "Touching is believing" and the image of the finger work together to reinforce the message that seeing the new object is not sufficient; the intimacy of touch is required to consummate the highly anticipated union between consumer and object of desire. At the literal level, the ad poses an equivalency between the sense of touch and the act of knowing.[15] The consumer is invited to touch the device in order to confirm its existence. This works as a reference to the prelaunch marketing hype for the iPhone. The feverish anticipation surrounding the launch is encoded in the image as the simple act of touching the new phone comes to represent the culmination of a union months in the making.

The phrase "Touching is believing" evokes the idiom "seeing is believing." While the ad copy works as a tongue-in-cheek reference to the uniqueness of the closely guarded product, a more mythological read reveals the epistemic shift that digital media favor. "Touching is believing," like "seeing is believing," describes a particular way of knowing. Seeing something is considered a privileged mode of determining reality or unreality. Aristotle claimed that sight gives us more knowledge and awareness than the other senses. The figures in Plato's cave were plagued by shadows that inhibited their ability to recognize the light.[16]

The Apple ad shows that the nature of knowing in the visual age has shifted. When images are subject to digital manipulation, it is more difficult to make claims about the authenticity of an image. This condition is exaggerated by digital imaging technologies that allow for the rapid dissemination (and potential distortion) of images. In this way, the caption in the iPhone ad makes a statement about the literal features of the product (a touchscreen) as well as the epistemic conditions of life in the age of the ever-present screen, an age in which the authenticity of screen images is constantly being called into question. The iPhone adds a tactile layer of expression to the information universe by incorporating the sense of touch and inviting the user to transcend the knowledge that comes from sight alone. "Seeing is believing" gives way to "Touching is believing."

Consumers are invited to seek what is true by touching screens that unlock libraries of knowledge in a matter of seconds. In *The Rhetoric of Religion*, Kenneth Burke writes, " '[T]echnologism' is a 'religion' to the extent that technology is viewed as an intrinsic good, so that its underlying, unspoken assumption is: 'The more technology, the higher the culture.' "[17] If one is disconnected from the flow of digital information, then the human need for social connection and information acquisition is amputated and the individual is left senseless, blind, deaf, dumb—unable to access the vital knowledge contained in the realm of infinite digital information.

The iPhone ad presents the phone as a hovering object, suspended over a sea of black, created ex nihilo, "out of nothing." The hand, with one finger extended, ready to touch the glowing body of the iPhone, is visually resonant with Michelangelo's iconography of the biblical creation account, evoking the "Creation of Adam" image that makes up part of Michelangelo's magnificent fresco in the Sistine Chapel. In the fresco, the figure of God reaches out to touch man, the crown of creation.[18]

Through the arrangement of signifiers in the ad, the reader is invited to more fully consider the phenomenological act of mediated communion. A creative tension emerges from the small space between the human finger and the glowing machine. One is reminded of the iconic image of the young boy reaching out to touch the glowing finger of ET in the 1982 Hollywood film. The use of touch speaks to a level of intimate contact that no other sense can provide. AT&T's use of the tagline "reach out and touch someone" speaks to this essential feature of human communion and its usefulness for telecommunications marketers. However, in true postmodern fashion, the act of touching is only a simulation that drives a finely tuned, graphics-based user interface. The user touches nothing concrete other than a pane of glass. Nonetheless, a sense of omnipotence is granted to the user, who is able to use the device as a sort of remote control for everyday life. The fawning and reverence reserved for the miraculous objects of modern technology are directed not at the machines themselves but at their symbolic function as supernatural enhancements to the sacred practice of human communication. Supernatural in this sense is meant to draw attention to the fact that our use of such objects allows us to transcend and exceed natural or embodied forms of human communication like human speech and physical presence. This transformation is no small matter as it places us in contact with people and information that are discarnate, without bodies. It is when we take this condition for granted that we overlook the role technology plays in reordering social relationships in such a way that human presence and actual human touch are effaced by digital simulation.

While the ad evokes a number of Christian allusions, the polysemous text could also be read as a derivation of Buddhist and gnostic belief. Because the Buddhist or gnostic views the physical world and human bodies as the source of all suffering, the digital realm represents the liberation of the mind and spirit from the prison of the body. Given Steve Jobs' affinity for Eastern spirituality, one might make the case that this interpretation is more compelling. The power of the Apple brand and its rhetoric is the multiple resonances it embodies. The interplay of physical and metaphysical is highly influential in how modern communication technology gets imagined in popular discourse. Apple exemplifies this by depicting products in preternatural settings, abstracted from scenes of everyday life and placed in whitewashed, blacked out, or surrealist environments that speak directly to the sensory separation from time and space that occurs when one engages with Apple's immersive objects.

Rationalizing the Universe One App at a Time

Apple's success is based in part on its ability to transform the cold rationalism and research that goes into creating its products into the

68 mythical language of scientific magic and technological mysticism.[19] In the promotional rhetoric of the Apple computer company, the convergence of the technological and the religious reveals a persistent dialectic at work in the American imagination between rationalism and mysticism. The aim of scientific rationalism, spawned in the wake of the religious wars of the seventeenth century, was to disenchant the world. For Descartes and other leading thinkers of the era, "reason" was a necessary antidote for a society torn apart by religious difference. Mystery and magic led only to chaos. Scientific rationalism provided a sense of order and control.[20]

The fruit of scientific rationalism can be seen today in the proliferation of techniques and technologies that make it possible for humanity to tame nature and reduce or eliminate contingency. By eliminating contingency or attempting to control it, the capricious will of the universe is neutered and caged. The rationalist asserts that humans, enlightened and rational humans, should be arbiters and captains of their own destiny. In an ironic twist of history, it is technology that has filled the void of enchantment by offering users a share in mastering a universe drained of fables and mysteries.[21] Max Weber summarized the situation this way: "The disenchantment of the world . . . means that principally there are no mysterious incalculable forces that come into play, but rather, that one can, in principle, master all things by calculation."[22] Devices like the iPhone represent more than convenient communication objects; they are symbols of a collective drive to eliminate contingency further from experience and to inherit the power of the deity: being both omnipresent, everywhere at once, and omniscient, knowing all there is to know. The quasi-supernatural power of modern technology is derived from its seemingly limitless scope.[23]

One of the ways in which the iPhone rhetoric delivers this quasi-supernatural message is by highlighting the magical qualities of the device. In this sense, things have come full circle. One of the most popular tools we use for eliminating contingency and containing complexity is itself treated as a sacramental object in the technological order. In religious tradition, the sacramental object is something capable of mediating transcendence. Like rosaries and relics, powerful communication devices are mediators of the virtually infinite digital sphere.

The iPhone and its touchscreen interface engage the technological faithful at a heightened level of intimacy. The iPhone is not a cold and lifeless machine; it is an enchanted talisman, animated by touch. It mimics an encounter with the transcendent by mediating the infinite body of online information and communication possibilities. Text, voice, and video make others present in a condition of instant communication that borders on the telepathic and angelic. In a *New York Times* review of the iPhone 4S, David Pogue uses words like "mind-blowing" and "unbelievable" to describe a phone that "feels like magic."[24]

The themes outlined above—the disenchantment of rationalism and a lingering tendency to view technology as something magical or pseudo-religious—are combined in the Apple narrative in a way that is instructive for scholars of religion, communication, and technology. Technology advertising is rarely explicitly religious; instead, the rhetoric is cloaked in postmodern and parodic allusion that invites viewers to fill in the gaps by reassembling the scraps of cultural and religious mythologies that pepper the technological discourse.

One of the first television ads for the iPhone features a setup very similar to the "Touching is believing" print ad. The backdrop is a deep black. A close-up of the phone fills the center of the frame. For thirty seconds, the viewer is taken on a tour of the iPhone's diverse set of features. From watching a movie to making dinner reservations, everything is a touch or swipe away. The ad focuses on the device screen that occupies the majority of the phone's face. The shot provides the visual sensation of watching a screen (the phone) within a screen (the television). The disembodied hands that handle the device thus become a signifier for the "manipulability" of this form of digital media. The signifier of the hand challenges the convention that media devices are merely sight and sound experiences. They are things to be touched, held, and manipulated.

70   In the world of the iPhone, viewing a film becomes an occasion to immediately indulge a craving for seafood. During a film scene involving a murderous squid, the voiceover playfully intones "mmm . . . did someone say calamari?" Instantly, the screen of the phone changes to a map where the user is able to pinpoint the nearest seafood restaurant in an effort to satiate this impulsive desire. A couple of seconds later, the phone function is activated and the user is connecting with the restaurant. From initial biological response to contact with the restaurant, less than twenty seconds has elapsed. The iPhone is a catholicon for securing instant gratification.

The "catholic" or universal appeal of the object is a point worth considering. In the age of iPhone, there is a social obsession with efficiency via process and technology, and it is universal. Whether we own an iPhone or not, the ethic of speed and efficiency is built into nearly all of our cultural practices. Jacques Ellul points out, "Geographically and qualitatively, technique is universal in its manifestations. It is devoted, by nature and necessity, to the universal . . . it is becoming the universal language understood by all men."[25] Ellul comments on the sociological impact of technique as if it were something religious: "Technique, moreover, creates a bond between men. All those who follow the same technique are bound together in a tacit fraternity and all of them take the same attitude toward reality."[26]

Another way in which the iPhone advertising exhibits the religious resonance of life in a technological society is through the colonization of leisure, exemplified in the Apple ads featuring the multitude of downloadable apps available for the phone. Apps are individual software applications that allow iPhone users to accomplish specific tasks. There are apps that provide weather reports, others that provide driving directions, others that provide access to banking information, and so on. Over thirty billion apps have been downloaded from the "App Store."[27]

With hundreds of thousands of apps and counting, Apple would have us believe that there is an app for everything. The Apple website crows that there is "almost no limit to what your iPhone can do."[28] Categories include games, business, news, sports, health, reference, and travel. Apps are also available for the iPod and iPad. Unlike personal computing applications, mobile apps are useful in virtually any context: in a car, at the bank, on a subway. As such, the apps have the ability to add a layer of enhanced experience to any environment. Exercise apps count miles and calories that can then be uploaded to a website to track fitness progress. Some fitness apps are incorporating biofeedback measures like heart rate to further enhance the overall workout experience.

What Apple has managed to do with the iPhone and the App Store is create a realm of productivity that redefines the cultural practice of leisure. Devices like the Blackberry are seen as corporate productivity devices, while the iPhone is depicted as something more playful and imaginative. This is a trope that Apple initiated with the introduction of the first Macintosh in a predominantly business-oriented IBM world, and it still persists today. This is also where the technology as cult concept is most relevant.[29]

The religiosity of the Apple brand community can be traced to the function of the device in the lives of users and the way it is represented in the advertising. If the iPhone is not strictly used for the purposes of accomplishing business tasks but also delivers the types of leisure activities (movies, games, cooking, exercise) sought by members of the technological society, then its role in the lives of users is something quite profound. The iPhone is a virtual remote control device that plays a central role in the leisure activities of its users. Whether making restaurant reservations, texting or calling a friend, or tracking workout performance, the sophisticated iPhone provides a multitude of ways to wield the universal remote in a variety of situations that previously lacked technological intervention. No matter the situation, it seems there is an app for it.

In the "Shazam" app commercial, a pair of hands hold an iPhone and act out the scenario being presented by the announcer: "You know when you don't know what song is playing and it's driving you crazy?" The anonymous user in the spot points the iPhone toward a pulsating speaker. The iPhone recognizes the song and displays all of the information on-screen. The commercial concludes with the announcer reminding the viewer that the iPhone solves "life's dilemmas one app at a time." Like many of the iPhone commercials, the action takes place on a white background, devoid of context. The hands appear to be male but are generic enough to signify a pair of "everyhands." The hands denote a capable user and signify the way the device is to be used; by touching the screen, swiping with the fingers, and pressing the onscreen icons. These cues provide implicit instructions for viewers who may be unfamiliar with the iPhone's functionality. The hands are also a metonym for the user. A part, the hands, stands for the whole person.

The hands command and conduct the machine, not through a peripheral piece of hardware like a keyboard or mouse, but through the screen itself. The hands caress the mediated icons and images as if they were physical realities. Previously, the images on-screen required hardware to manipulate; now the hands make direct contact. This action of manipulation, the etymology of which refers directly to the hands, is one of creation, or in the case of the iPhone, re-creation. The passivity of traditional media experiences gives way to the creative activity of the hands that engage the elements on-screen.

The iPhone redefines traditional leisure activities. In the "Shazam" commercial, listening to a song, once an occasion for relaxation and pleasure, is portrayed as an occasion of anxiety because not knowing a song could be "driving us crazy." Knowing the name of the song signifies a form of ownership of that piece of culture. Furthermore, knowing the name of the song allows one literally to own the song by purchasing the artist's recording. The iPhone streamlines this consumer process by digitizing it. Figuring out the name of the song is no longer a task accomplished by calling the radio station or asking a friend, it is something accomplished by the omniscient iPhone. This leisure activity is no longer profitable in the humanistic sense of enjoying culture for its own sake. It is deemed profitable once an acquisition has been made, either the name of the song or a recording of the song, or both. The speed at which this is accomplished is also portrayed as profitable because it provides instant gratification.

The idea of an activity being profitable in the consumerist/technologist sense counters the view of culture that privileges the practice of unmediated contemplation. For modern philosophers like Josef Pieper, the contemplation of the true and the beautiful, directed by religious ritual and observance, is a kind of rest. This kind of rest, rooted in contemplative activity, is restorative and creative. This, says Pieper, is the basis of culture and human freedom, a view that has been lost in the sea of mediated consumption that demands constant action by the user and rejects stillness and silence.

What Apple offers us in the iPhone ads is a false freedom, one that offers amusement and efficiency as counterfeit forms of human leisure. The hands in the ad are the hands of a shackled individual, one who cannot engage the real world without consulting the virtual first. They are also hands without a head. The "user" surrenders his or her intellectual expansion to the songs, movies, games, and apps that now invade the last outposts of human contemplation in contemporary culture: a subway car on the way to work, a small table in a café, a cross-country automobile ride.

It is fitting that so many clamor for phones and entertainment devices in transit. The mobilization and privatization inaugurated by the motorcar are now made available in personal technology. The devices transport the user, temporarily, from reality. What we do in the moments once reserved for reflection and contemplation becomes a de facto religion of sorts. It fills in the gaps of silence and presents a world removed from the one we are in. It is a form of existential escape. Religion, it seems, can be easily aped. By colonizing leisure, the iPhone, like the computer before it, stakes its claim as one of the bases of the technological culture.

Reading the Religion of Technology

The religion of technology bears some resemblance to Protestant eschatology.[30] From the half-eaten Apple logo, a figure for the forbidden fruit in the Garden of Eden, to the Orwellian vision of a fallen planet of IBM drones, the Apple rhetoric seems to be saying that the earth is a fallen place and that the tools of science and technology grant us the ability to redeem and ultimately perfect our fallen state of being on the path to perfection. It grants us power over our surroundings in ways that were previously unthinkable. David Noble notes that developments like the atomic bomb and genetic engineering speak to both the creative and destructive ways in which creatures seek to imitate the creator.

The iPhone is not atomic, but it is emblematic of what Albert Einstein called the information bomb.[31] The radioactivity of nuclear weaponry precedes the interactivity wrought by telecommunications technology. The explosion of information and digital computing has infiltrated all aspects of social and cultural life. The "fallout" of interactivity induces a radical mutation of work habits and social interaction. Ingrained patterns of social and cultural life are remade in the image and likeness of the machines that have become the new nature. In the Protestant eschatological view, this development is a positive step toward human perfection, making us more godlike by imitating omniscience and omnipresence, if only in a virtual sense. French philosopher Paul Virilio noticed a similar parallel between religion and technology:

> The new technologies bring into effect the three traditional characteristics of the Divine: ubiquity, instantaneity and immediacy. Without some cultural familiarity with these themes, mediated by Christianity, Protestantism, Buddhism, Judaism, Islam, etc., they remain incomprehensible. One cannot come to grips with the phenomenon of cyberspace without some inkling of, or some respect for, metaphysical intelligence! That does not mean that you have to be converted. I believe that the new technologies demand from those who are interested in them that they have a substantial measure of religious culture and not merely some religious opinion.[32]

In the modern age, religious beliefs are viewed as relative equals permitting seekers to experiment with and dabble in competing systems. The various systems, be they Christian, Buddhist, Muslim, new age, or otherwise, are now "open source," to use the parlance of computer programmers. Apple's Steve Jobs made it a point to read his favorite book, *Autobiography of a Yogi*, once a year. The book was written by Indian spiritual guru Paramahansa Yogananda, a man credited with bringing yoga and meditation to the West in the 1920s. The book is filled with a synthetic blend of Hindu and Christian teachings along with stories of miracles and saints. In 2008 Jobs personally telephoned the Self-Realization Foundation, run by Yogananda's devotees, to request permission to sell *Autobiography of a Yogi* on iTunes. In 2011, the year Jobs passed away, the only book on his iPad for what turned out to be his last family trip to Hawaii was *Autobiography of a Yogi*.

For a man who did not finish college and never formally studied computer science or industrial design, Jobs drew many of his inspired ideas from elsewhere. Yogananda was known for teaching Kriya Yoga, a spiritual science for achieving union with God. The science of divine union is rooted in a series of techniques that require intense concentration and promise a profound religious experience. Jobs' desire to combine the humanities with engineering in his products resonates with the idea that religious experiences are something that can be programmed through technique. It fulfills the insight of Swiss psychiatrist Carl Jung, who said, "When a religious method recommends itself as 'scientific,' it can be certain of its public in the West."[33] The inverse may also be true. The marriage of physics and metaphysics in the Apple rhetoric is symptomatic of the enduring relationship between a culture's crowning technological achievements and questions of ultimate concern.

4

Technology and Religion
Where the Physical and Metaphysical Meet

In a diary published after his death, American artist Andy Warhol remembers a man persistently calling to offer him a free Macintosh computer. Warhol never called the man back. Months later, Warhol met the magnanimous mystery caller at John Lennon's apartment on West Seventy-Second Street in New York. The man calling Warhol was Steve Jobs, and both were at a party for Sean Lennon's ninth birthday. Jobs naturally brought the birthday boy a Macintosh.

Warhol walked in on Jobs showing young Sean how to use the Macintosh paint program. Crude by today's standards, MacPaint allowed the user to draw lines on the screen in black and white. Warhol asked if he could try the new machine and clumsily waved the mouse in the air. Jobs showed him that the mouse worked by moving it along a surface. Once Warhol got the hang of it, he was transfixed. "Look! Keith! I drew a circle!" he announced to artist friend Keith Haring. He spent the rest of the night glued to the computer.[1]

There is little doubt Steve Jobs was delighted to see his new machine in the hands of a famed American artist. The meeting between Jobs, prophet of technology, and Warhol, iconographer of consumerism, was immortalized in Roberto Parada's illustration for *Playboy* magazine. A haloed Jobs delivers the transcendent Macintosh in a cardboard manger in the presence of a robed Warhol, Walter Cronkite (also at the Lennon birthday party), and John Lennon in a St. Michael the archangel pose. In the background, the cherubic Sean Lennon peers over his late father's outstretched wing (see facing page). The archetypal scene is doused with parody as the Christ child is no longer a child at all, but a machine. Rather than God becoming man, the code becomes Mac.[2]

Like much of the promotional discourse surrounding the Apple brand, Parada's parody of the birth of Macintosh provides a number of intertextual allusions.[3] The familiar symbols of mangers, angels, and shepherds add to Apple's religious mythos and also invite an allegorical reading of media and art in the age of transcendent machines. In the illustration, Cronkite represents media's old guard, bemused and a bit perplexed by the device that is about to revolutionize the traditional media environment. The establishment's authoritative voice declaring "and that's the way it is" was about to give way to a cacophony of digital voices publishing and broadcasting themselves. If the power of the press belongs to those who own one, the Macintosh would multiply that power exponentially.

Warhol plays the role of the prophet Simeon in the New Testament account of Jesus' presentation in the temple. When Jesus is presented to the temple authorities in the Mosaic ritual of the redemption of the firstborn, Simeon recognizes the infant as Israel's messiah, a revelation that he prayed he would receive before he died. Warhol is the Simeon of the art world. The prophet of the pop art movement died two years after completing a series of Macintosh logo screen prints in his trademark style (see p. 80). In the presence of Jobs and his machine, Warhol recognizes in a fit of awe the future of popular art production in the Macintosh.

John Lennon peers over the scene, the archangel of the creative class, silently standing guard between this world and the next, prepared to vanquish those who threaten Apple's messianic destiny. His

Roberto Parada,
"The Night Steve Jobs Met Andy Warhol"

Andy Warhol,
"Apple Macintosh"
from the Ads Suite

eyes are not fixed on the sublimities of heaven but on the machinations of the inventors and artists below. The computer sits in the place of the archetypal Christ child in the manger. Humanity's savior is no longer human at all, but a technological commodity. The substitution of computer for Creator in the scene is reminiscent of Jacques Ellul's assertion that "the mysterious is merely that which has not yet been technicized."[4]

The religious depiction of Jobs and Warhol in the image is a metonym for the meeting of art, technology, and religion. Artists like Warhol have the ability to herald the major cultural shifts that result from the introduction of new technologies.[5] American literary critic and poet Ezra Pound said, "[I]t is the business of the artist to make humanity aware of itself."[6] This becomes especially true in the times of technological upheaval. For instance, James Joyce conveyed the psychic and social changes being wrought by early mass media in his cryptic and playful use of sound and language in *Ulysses* and *Finnegans Wake*.[7] The pointillist painters of the late nineteenth century created images that prefigured the pixelated screens of today. Art has the ability to signal coming changes in ways that stir those who are aware of such things from their slumber.

Media theorist Marshall McLuhan was fond of poet Ezra Pound's dictum that artists are the "antennae of the race." McLuhan interpreted it to mean that artists are the ones best equipped to describe the changes in the cultural environment wrought by new technology. While the artist's work remains obscure at first, over time it reveals an attempt to provide an "anti-environment" to the one in which the rest of us are unconsciously immersed.[8] In the case of Warhol, the screen-printed celebrities and consumer products draw upon cultural critic Walter Benjamin's notion that the "aura" or sacred uniqueness is dispelled when images and objects are mass produced.[9] Warhol's work presages the empty idolatry of fame and consumption of the late twentieth century. In the case of technology, religion scholar J. Sage Elwell argues that much of avant-garde digital art depicts a world that has lost a sense of transcendence. To discern the moral and spiritual

82 changes wrought by technology, Elwell points out, one need look no
further than the arts—where a culture's spiritual impulses are put on
display. The art and technology of late modernity seem to symbolize
the erosion of transcendence taking place in the technological, con-
sumerist environment.

The visionary status of artists is derived in part from the religious
traditions from which they draw their inspiration. In a 1985 interview,
Jobs asked,

> What are we, anyway? Most of what we think we are is just a
> collection of likes and dislikes, habits, patterns. At the core of
> what we are is our values, and what decisions and actions we
> make reflect those values.[10]

Jobs may or may not have read the work of the French historian
Alexis de Tocqueville in his lifetime, but Tocqueville's sentiments
are similar. Tocqueville spent some time traveling America in the
nineteenth century to get a sense for the culture of the place. In one
reflection, he writes,

> There is hardly any human action, however particular it may
> be, that does not originate in some very general idea men
> have conceived of the Deity, of his relation to mankind, of the
> nature of their own souls, and of their duties to their fellow
> creatures. Nor can anything prevent these ideas from being the
> common spring from which all the rest emanates.[11]

While Jobs opts for the humanist language of "values," Tocqueville
points out that our ideas and values are ultimately derived from our
relation to God.

In the years following Warhol's death, more knowledge about his
secret piety came to the surface. Warhol attended Mass several times
a week on New York's Upper West Side. His visual style was clearly
influenced by the iconostasis, the rows and rows of gold-leafed icons
that adorned the front of St. John Chrysostom Byzantine Catholic

Iconostasis in Trinity Cathedral, Ipatiev Monastery, Russia

Andy Warhol, "Marilyn" series

iPad Interface

84   Church in Pittsburgh, Pennsylvania (for an example of iconostasis, see p. 83, top), where as a youth he would spend up to eight hours a week with his mother attending Mass.[12] The replication of images in Warhol's work (p. 83, middle) has been seen by some as an imitation of the universal structures of Catholicism:[13]

> Through the ritual of art, Warhol proclaims their glory through a mass of detail, monotonously intoning their holy names even unto the heavenly infinity inherent in the grid or serial format. The same thing, over and over again, in whatever direction, stretching away, infinitely.[14]

Warhol's religious imagination, formed on iconography, is manifest in his work. Jobs and Warhol belong next to each other in such a discussion because they both epitomize the collision of technology and popular art. Insofar as art and technology are sites where the physical and metaphysical meet, the metaphysical framework of the artist inevitably influences his or her physical artistry.

Engineering Enlightenment

Just as art provides a fruitful site for exploring the intersection of the physical and the metaphysical, engineering, an art in its own right, serves a similar function. As teenagers, Jobs and Apple cofounder Steve Wozniak belonged to a group of electronics hobbyists known as "wireheads." Tinkering with electronics at that time was considered a "cool" hobby and was more sophisticated than just being a marijuana-smoking "pothead." Wozniak was obsessed with electronics, and it was a hobby that kept him out of trouble in the turbulent, drug-fueled seventies. Wozniak remembers, "I was lucky. Keys to happiness came to me that would keep me happy for the whole of my life. It was just accidental. I don't know how many people get it. It's like a religion or something that just popped into my head, walking home from school."[15] As a thirteen-year-old, Wozniak received his eureka moment while studying an adder-subtractor circuit in a trade magazine: "[H]e understood not only how the circuit worked but its underlying metaphysics."[16] It was at this point that Wozniak realized electronics could "create the world itself; becoming thought and memory. It could inhabit a universe of its own devising."[17]

Wozniak's sheltered teenage years were drastically different from the years of freewheeling experimentation of his future business partner, Steve Jobs. The availability of LSD and marijuana in northern California meant that electronics and drugs became intertwined hobbies for some wireheads. Hobbyists and engineers alike realized they were able better to design the minds of machines by tinkering with their own minds. The partnership of Wozniak and Jobs was the perfect marriage of engineering prowess with spiritual insight.

After dropping out of Reed College and working for Atari at night, Jobs explored Eastern spirituality by traveling to India with his friend, Dan Kottke. While Wozniak continued to tinker, Jobs became more interested in the "electric atmosphere of love" reported by his friend Robert Friedland while studying the teachings of Indian guru Neem Karoli Baba. In India, Jobs took on the role of a mendicant, a spiritual beggar who depends on the kindness of strangers. He traveled from Delhi to the Himalayas, where he shaved his head and participated in various Hindu rituals.[18]

Jobs became somewhat disillusioned as he met different gurus who tried to impart ideas about the essence of existence, but it did not dampen his search for enlightenment. It was not until the end of the journey, when he and Kottke were trying to find shelter from a driving thunderstorm, that anything close to a religious experience took place. The two men, digging in the sand of a dry creek bed to escape the lightning and rain, called out to God, promising to be good people if they survived. After reflecting on his intense and disturbing pilgrimage, Jobs recalled, "It was one of the first times that I started to realize that maybe Thomas Edison did a lot more to improve the world than Karl Marx and Neem Karoli Baba put together."[19]

When Jobs returned to America, he experienced a sense of culture shock. His parents did not recognize him when they came to pick him up at the airport. Jobs was dressed in long, flowing cotton robes, and his head was shaved. By stepping outside the West, he came to believe that Western ways of thinking were problematic and that the Western mind was crazy. People in the West were obsessed with dealing with their past, planning for the future, and amassing as many material possessions as possible. Jobs was convinced that enlightenment was found by remaining in the present, shedding attachment to material things and rewiring the mind to accept intuition over rationality as the road to wisdom.

Steve Jobs felt that his experience in India had a major impact on his work. The power of intuition captivated him, so much so that it became the hallmark of his product design and philosophy. He found the most striking examples of intuitive thought and experiential wisdom among the illiterate Hindu villagers who served as hosts and guides on his journey. It became clear to Jobs that his calling was to develop tools for the mind that would deprogram the Western mentality of linear rationality and formal logic. For Jobs, rationality and logic were products of a print world that was now taking a backseat to the nonlinear world of digital information. In the digital age, books would surrender to bits. The computer world would need an enlightened guru for the conversion, which was about to take place.

In 1975 Jobs' search for truth was still not satisfied. He was back at Atari and began exploring Zen Buddhism more deeply. He ate only fruit, fasted, and attended meditation retreats at the nearby Los Altos Zen Center. Jobs liked the fact that Zen had no "religious structure" and was instead a self-directed spirituality that emphasized "experience, intuition, and self-fulfillment through inner consciousness."[20] It was at this time that Jobs met Japanese Zen master Kobun Chino. Jobs' friend Kottke recalls a particular exchange at the Zen master's house where the three men were sitting, talking, and drinking tea: "All of a sudden, Steve says to Kobun, 'What do you think of speed? You know, doing things fast?' He was really serious about it and was really into this idea that the quicker you could do something, the better a person you were."[21]

The transition from the analog age to the digital age brought about by computing would change not only the way we thought about machines but also how we thought about ourselves. It would take a techno-spiritual guru to convert the heady morass of memory chips, downloads, and bandwidth into terms that average consumers could understand. Jobs was well suited for the job. Jobs employed the power of myth and metaphor—literary devices common to religious rhetoric—to capture the imagination of a public not yet sold on the idea of a computer in every home. Jobs debunked the idea that computers were intimidating devices for Cold War code breakers and pencil-necked mathematicians; instead, he positioned them as tools for transcending stale traditions and re-enchanting the world.

During the run-up to the 1984 Macintosh computer launch, Jobs had the following exchange with marketing director Mike Murray:

"We don't stand a chance of advertising with features and benefits and with RAMs and with charts and comparisons," Jobs said.

"The only chance we have of communicating is with a feeling."

"It's got to be like a Sony Walkman or a Cuisinart. It's got to be a cult product," Murray said.

"Yeah, we say, it's a cult, and then we say, hey, drink this Kool-Aid." He strolled to the door and said, "We want to create an image people will never forget. We've got to build it, and we've got to build it early."[22]

The result was the infamous "1984" ad, in which the "IBM society" (depicted as Orwellian) is demolished by the rebellious Macintosh movement. By correlating the "business machine" computer culture with all that is depersonalizing and soulless in society, Apple managed to create an image and a feeling about computers that was liberating rather than confining. The feeling generated by the ad was contagious.

The Apple movement is not a cult maintained by high priests and secret oaths, it is a self-directed body (true to the Zen spirituality of the company's founder) that inspires Mac fanatics to evangelize for the cause. Apple's strategy is merely to keep them around, keep them happy, and allow them to do the evangelizing. In the how-to management book *The Apple Way*, author Jeffrey Cruikshank advises that "you don't have to get everybody to join the cult. You just have to get the smartest, most connected, and most committed people to sign up. (Think Opus Dei.) They'll do the rest."[23]

The Zen Buddhism of Steve Jobs is self-directed, self-important, and skeptical of rational analysis. Zen is about intuition and spontaneity. Apple devices allow the users to "self-direct" their experience, whether it is through personalized playlists on the iPod or customized interfaces on the iMac. The Apple machines eschew clunky interfaces for elegant, one-button designs with touchscreens that appeal to intuition. Apple has created the machines to which uninitiated computer users gravitate for ease of use and intuitive design. During the development of the Apple II, Jobs decided the computer should have no fan because it needed to be quiet. Jobs believed that customers would appreciate a computer that did not make lots of machine noise. His conviction arose from his study of Zen meditation, where noise was something that impeded mental and spiritual growth.[24]

As discussed, the ad campaign for the first iPhone was about spontaneity: a device that could show a feature film, get directions to a seafood restaurant, and then place a call to the restaurant in less than thirty seconds. Intuition, speed, and spontaneity are hallmarks of Apple and stem in part from the founder's formative experiences in Eastern mysticism that continue to inform Apple's corporate and consumer culture.

Computer companies founded by technicians, engineers, and savvy executives derive their strength and sustainability from quality products and good marketing. Companies like Apple possess the rare ability to create quality products, market them well, and formulate a social philosophy that transcends the business. Steve Jobs helped create a company that uses its tools as metaphors for professing what is good about digital culture. At a time when our device lifestyle breeds Internet addiction, hollow relationships, and short attention spans,

Jobs' company proposes romantic notions of self-fulfillment in the form of enlightened machines. The entire digital ecosystem benefits from this philosophical coup. If technology can be imagined in the spirit of higher consciousness, creative discovery, and greater self-awareness, then it becomes a social good. It escapes the prejudice that fettered early computers characterized by esoteric programming languages and dubious military projects. The cold military computer and impersonal business machine that focused on raw computation and data storage bore no traces of the human spirit and imagination that were part of its creation.

The mythos popularized by Apple found its way into the rhetoric of other communication technology companies as well. Verizon's tagline in 2011 was "Rule the Air" (see p. 90, top). The mythic tone of this slogan conjures images of Greek gods or something darker. In the Bible, Satan is referred to as "prince and power of the air" (Ephesians 2:2). In one of the Verizon television ads for their 4G cellular service, a thunderstorm awakens a young man in the middle of the night. He jumps out of bed, grabs his laptop, and heads into the street, where a tree has been split by a violent lightning strike. The visual tone is dark and foreboding as he approaches the tree and finds a Verizon 4G access card (a device used for wireless Internet access) lodged in the tree's severed trunk. The ad implies that the miraculous manifestation of the access card was a result of the lightning strike. The connotation is that the access card is as fast and powerful as lightning. Keeping in mind the brand tagline "Rule the Air," the scene can also be read as another biblical metaphor. The "fruit" of the tree (the access card) offers the young man infinite access to online knowledge—not unlike the fruit of the tree of knowledge that the Apple logo connotes as well.

The man partakes of the tree by pulling the access card from the burnt trunk and plugging it into his laptop. His face is illuminated by the screen of his computer and bears an expression of awe at his new discovery, giving him godlike access, omniscient and omnipresent, to the universe of online information. It is reminiscent of Apple's

Verizon "Rule the Air" ad campaign

AT&T "Rethink Possible" ad campaign

"1984" ad in which the light streams forth and illuminates the faces of formerly ignorant "PC" masses. The ad ends with Verizon's unintentionally diabolical tagline, "Rule the Air." Very few consumers understand the particulars of how information is transmitted over the electromagnetic spectrum, so the mythic treatment provides a more universal appeal.

An AT&T ad asks the viewer to "Rethink Possible." The dramatic images in the AT&T ad show enormous gauzy drapes falling on major cities and landmarks, captivating onlookers who stand mouths agape at the grand spectacle (see facing page, bottom, as an example). The message is focused on coverage, meaning radio signal coverage for cell phones. The ability to transmit from anywhere, from the top of the Gateway Arch in St. Louis to the bottom of the Hoover Dam, is promoted as an inherent good.

The ad suggests that AT&T, or communication technology, has become the new "technological sublime." In an earlier era of American ingenuity, one might have stood in awe at the manmade magnificence of architectural accomplishments. However, in the age of speed-of-light communication, these monumental artifacts seem pedestrian. The power to harness the air (and its electromagnetic spectrum) above and around these monuments becomes the ultimate act of transcendence. Their size and grandeur are superseded by the all-encompassing "network." This is symbolized by orange blankets that envelop the landscape and cover the sacred monuments to American progress. The enveloping nature of modern technology is visually connected to earth's primordial nature in the closing scene. At the end of the commercial, dozens of jubilant people carry the orange gauzy blanket to the edge of the sea, a tableau that connotes AT&T's presence as oceanic, vast and deep. The aesthetic quality of the ad and the contemplative soundtrack sanctify the process of digital coverage as if the areas being draped are somehow christened by AT&T's omnipresence.

The most iconic ads of the Jobs era are not mere marketing messages; they are imaginative myths designed to re-enchant technological

92 objects. The ads for Apple's iPad 3 reflect this mythological leaning. In one promotional video, the narrator intones,

> We believe technology is at its very best when it's invisible—when you're conscious only of what you're doing, not the device you're doing it with. An iPad is the perfect expression of that idea. It's just this magical pane of glass that can become anything you want it to be. And that's why so many people in so many different places are using it for so many different things. It's a more personal experience with technology than people have ever had. . . . We think it's going to change how you see and do just about everything.

The inclusion of the invisible and the magical connotes something mythic. The inner workings of the iPad are invisible to the user. Most users are largely unaware and uninterested in the function of the circuits and chips that power the device. The user operates the device on faith, trusting that it will dutifully follow commands. The less resistance the device provides, the less we think about what we are actually using.

While the content of the media stimulates the conscious mind, the device itself, if designed well, operates at the level of the subconscious. In a movie theater, the audience forgets about the projector and operator and gets lost in the screen. The moment we become conscious of the "inner workings" is the moment the magic of the experience fades. The more intuitive and seamless the interface, the less conscious the user becomes of the technology itself. Experiencing the "magical pane of glass" becomes natural and effortless. Impulses for seeking visual stimulation are satisfied immediately and intuitively—much like dreaming.

Jobs claimed to read *Autobiography of a Yogi* at least once a year.[25] In the book, the Indian spiritual guru Paramahansa Yogananda writes, "At night man enters the state of dream-consciousness and escapes from the false egotistic limitations that daily hem him round. In sleep he has an ever recurrent demonstration of the omnipotence of his mind. Lo! in the dream appear his long-dead friends, the remotest continents, the resurrected scenes of his childhood."[26] In the iPad ad we hear that the magical pane of glass can become anything we want it to be. It offers us omnipotence, a genie-in-the-bottle sort of experience that can, like dreams, conjure images of friends and faraway places or scenes from memory. The computer provides an electronic substitute for dream consciousness—a continuous flow of images, familiar and foreign, directed by the dreamer.

According to the great yogi, "Intuition is soul guidance, appearing naturally in man during those instants when his mind is calm. . . . The human mind, freed from the disturbances or 'static' of restlessness, is empowered to perform all the functions of complicated radio mechanisms—sending as well as receiving thoughts, and tuning out undesirable ones."[27] As the iPad ad tells us, the best technology is invisible, it allows us to focus only on what we are doing. The yogi uses a radio metaphor to describe the ideal spiritual state—one free of distraction. In a creative inversion, Apple uses analogies of consciousness to promote media technology, while the Indian mystic Yogananda uses analogies of media technology to promote higher consciousness.

At the 2010 introduction of the iPad, Apple's lead designer, Jonathan Ive, said, "[W]hen something exceeds your ability to understand how it works, it . . . becomes magical. And that's exactly what the iPad is." This rhetorical formula is a fixture in the Apple story. The consumer is not expected to understand the underlying physics or code that makes a computer work. This adds to the mystery of a machine that functions . . . magically.

Another of Jobs' favorite esoteric interests was the book *Be Here Now*, by Baba Ram Dass. In the book, psychiatrist Richard Alpert, who pioneered many of the first LSD studies in the United States, recounts his travels to India and his subsequent spiritual awakening. While in India, Alpert discarded his American identity and became Baba Ram Dass. The book had a profound and transformative effect on Jobs and his friends. Jobs felt that the book's spiritual insights, combined with meditation and drugs like LSD, provided the keys to a new sense of identity, a new consciousness, and a new way of seeing the world—a way to "think different."

When Albert Hoffman was studying ergot fungus in 1943, he had no way of predicting that the chemical he discovered, lysergic acid diethylamide, would become the catalyst for a cultural revolt nearly twenty years later. By the time countercultural heroes Timothy Leary, Ken Kesey, and Baba Ram Dass got their hands on LSD, a cult movement had formed and the new states of consciousness were just an acid trip away. Psychedelic pioneers believed that they were "storming heaven,"[28] as their forays into hallucinated worlds had all the marks of a religious mystical experience. Baba Ram Dass expressed a strong need to "socialize this thing about the new states of consciousness."[29] Timothy Leary would later say that the personal computer was the LSD of the 1990s. For Jobs, socializing the new consciousness would not come by way of illegal drugs, but by personal technology.

Steve Jobs had a keen sense for mythologizing technology. For Jobs, technology was more than a tool, it was a way to elevate consciousness. His forays into Zen Buddhism and LSD informed this technological philosophy. Like drugs and spirituality, technology provides a means for mediating the world. It has a transformative potential in its ability to induce new states of perception. Putting on a pair of iPod earbuds can transform a person's mood and perception of one's surroundings. The right song at the right moment can start a flood of endorphins—the sort of feel-good high that mimics a chemical or mystical experience. Apple devices are more than storage capacity and processor speed; they are tools for seeking a lost sense of transcendence.

Conclusion

The Paradox of Technological Belief

American Progress

The image that opens this chapter is an 1872 oil painting by artist John Gast called "American Progress." It is an allegory for the modernization of the American West. Such imagery was part of the national belief in Manifest Destiny—the idea that the westward expansion of American government and infrastructure was preordained by God to serve as a new heaven on earth.[1] In the image, the goddess Columbia, a popular female personification of the United States, leads her sons westward while laying a trail of telegraph wire to connect the new country. The people below, from left to right, travel on horseback, in wagons, and on trains and ships, signifying the progress of transportation technology in America.

Note that people guide the material modes of transportation, but a goddess carries the telegraph. This new form of transport made possible by the telegraph, the metaphysical transmission of thought over wires at the speed of electricity, is depicted by a spiritual metaphor. The presence of spiritual metaphor in technological rhetoric is not something unique to the Apple story but is part of an enduring cultural fascination with electronic communication. The promethean potential of electricity was enchanting to nineteenth-century Americans. Samuel Morse christened the first commercial telegraph line from Baltimore to Washington with a Bible verse from the book of Numbers, "What hath God wrought?"[2] An anonymous telegraph enthusiast of the same era had this to say:

> The most remarkable effect [of the telegraph], if I may judge from my own narrow thought, will be the approach to a practical unity of the human race; of which we have never yet had a foreshadowing, except in the Gospel of Christ.[3]

This characterization of new technology was not uncommon and has not entirely disappeared in our own time. Danny Hillis, a pioneering computer scientist in the early 1990s, described the coming revolution thusly:

Telephony, computers, and CD-ROMs are all specialized
mechanisms we've built to bind us together. . . . We are not
evolution's ultimate product. There's something coming after
us, and I imagine it is something wonderful. But we may never
be able to comprehend it, any more than a caterpillar can comprehend turning into a butterfly.[4]

The "mechanisms we've built to bind us together" evoke the etymology of the word "religion," "to bind fast."[5]

The image and rhetoric above suggest a mythic inevitability
about the social and spiritual benefits of new technology. But it is not
inevitable that a new technology, no matter how useful or interesting, will survive, let alone spark a tremendous cultural transformation.
When Ken Olsen, founder of the Digital Equipment Corporation, said
in 1977 "there is no reason anyone would want a computer in their
home," he was only echoing what IBM president Thomas Watson said
thirty years prior: "I think there is a world market for maybe five computers." When the executives at Xerox squashed their own personal
computer project in the late 1970s, they did so because of a disconnect
between the hippie West Coast researchers in their R&D department
and the East Coast marketing and sales execs (the executives from
Xerox's Connecticut headquarters did not care for the beanbag chairs
and laid-back management style of the company's Palo Alto lab).

The popularization of the first personal computer, with a mouse,
icons, and pull-down menus, was taken up by a twenty-four-year-old
Steve Jobs. When Jobs visited Xerox PARC in 1979, he believed he
had seen the future of computing. Jobs took the user interface ideas he
saw, hired several of the PARC researchers, and produced the Macintosh five years later. Meanwhile, the Xerox executives remained stuck
on the idea that they were only in the office copier business.[6]

What set Jobs apart from the myopic executives at Xerox was his
ability to educate the public about personal computing in both practi-
cal and mythic terms. Apple's advertisements are allegorical in their
orientation. They are rhetorical attempts to domesticate the foreign

and abstract concepts native to computer science, making them accessible and attractive to everyday adherents. The personal computer was not just about an improved user interface and a smaller motherboard. The personal computer signaled an epochal shift that would rival that of the print and electronic (telegraph, radio, TV, film) revolutions. The shift would require a fitting mythology—a coherent narrative for understanding the transcendent possibilities of networked computing.

The implications of such a shift are far-reaching because the new literacy brings about a noetic change, a change in patterns of thinking.[7] When the dominant modes of communication change, so do the metaphysical frameworks for religious belief.[8] The connection between forms of mediation and modes of belief is as old as the spoken word. Judaism, Christianity, and Islam, all religions of the book, were able to take root and spread as a result of the communication changes that facilitated their growth. As happened during the time of Jesus and St. Paul, when writing transformed the oral cultures of Europe and the Mediterranean, the invention of the printing press was a pivotal historical event that helped reshape the religious landscape in the fifteenth century.

An ancient Egyptian myth helps illuminate the perennial relationship between media forms and metaphysical belief systems. In a story about the introduction of writing to Egyptian culture, the Egyptian god Theuth visits King Thamus to show him that writing "once learned, will make the Egyptians wiser and will improve their memory."[9] Thamus replies by admonishing Theuth that his affection for writing prevents him from acknowledging its pitfalls. Writing does not improve memory but makes students more forgetful because they stop internalizing information. Writing also exposes students to ideas without requiring careful contemplation, meaning they will have "the appearance of wisdom" without true knowledge.[10] The celebration of technological values in the Apple story requires a similar response. The technological values promoted by Apple are part of the Faustian bargain of technology, which giveth and taketh away.[11]

A story about the Waldorf School in northern California is illustrative of the tension raised by new information technologies. At the Waldorf School of the Peninsula, the classrooms still have chalkboards, wooden desks, encyclopedias, and number 2 pencils. Students learn math skills by knitting and baking. Language skills come from reciting verses while catching beanbags. Computers and other forms of media technology are conspicuously absent from the school situated in the heart of Silicon Valley. For the Waldorf set, dividing and eating pieces of cake trumps learning virtual fractions on a computer screen. Ironically, many of the parents who send their children to Waldorf are executives at Apple, Google, Yahoo!, and Hewlett-Packard. They are among a growing number of technology leaders who have become more reflective about their own technological products.[12]

Silicon Valley parents insulating their children from the technologies that their companies create is both ironical and paradoxical. It seems that those most closely aligned with the technological order have also had to adopt a series of adaptive techniques for living in a technology-saturated environment. Incessant messaging and online media consumption can be mentally exhausting. So yoga, monastic retreats, technology fasts, and alternative schools have become fashionable escapes for the digerati overwhelmed by electronic stimuli. The Wisdom 2.0 conference held annually in California invites Silicon Valley participants to learn techniques for living with "greater presence, meaning, and mindfulness in the technology age."[13]

Steve Jobs' spiritual seeking was not unique, but a symptom of a much broader cultural concern—the realization that personal technology as an extension of the human mind also poses a threat to contemplative wisdom. King Thamus' anxieties about the new media of writing threatening wisdom have been resurrected in digital form. But Steve Jobs never lost his inner Buddhist monk. Jobs confronted the technology paradox by adhering to the tenets of Eastern spirituality as a means of imagining technology as a tool for expanding human consciousness rather than as a means of escape from it.

100   The tension between technology and spirituality was not a zero-sum game for Jobs. His Zen master Kobun Chino told him that he "could keep in touch with his spiritual side while running a business."[14] In true Zen fashion, Jobs avoided thinking of technology and spirituality in dualistic terms. Jobs' famous decision to manufacture computers without cooling fans was made to allow the user to achieve a Zen-like concentration, undistracted by the machine's noise. Jobs envisioned technology and spiritual practice as complementary, both contributing to human flourishing.

The iconography of the Apple computer company, the advertisements, and the device screens of the Macintosh, iPod, iPhone, and iPad are visual expressions of Jobs' imaginative marriage of spiritual science and modern technology. Apple's advertising, like all advertising, performs a vital educational function in consumer society. Technology ads provide parables and proverbs for navigating the complexities of the new technological order. They instruct the consumer on how to live the "good life" in the technological age.

The ads of the Apple computer company resemble medieval morality plays in their personification of good (Mac) and evil (PC). As such, they contain a moral, or, more explicitly, they propose a morality customized for the conditions of the age. Media technology has acquired a moral status because it has become part of the natural order of things. Luddites, those who have sworn off new technologies, are the new heretics and illiterates. Technology is an absolute. There is no turning back or imagining a different social order. Challenge is acceptable as long as it remains within the confines of the technological order. Apple may challenge Microsoft. Samsung may challenge Apple. But the order must not be challenged.

The impact of digital culture, then, is epistemic; it insinuates a moral system based on its own internal logic. The underlying message of the Mac versus PC ads is not simply that the Apple operating system is superior to that of Microsoft. The ads carry the implicit assertion that technology always means human progress. In addition, the personification of the operating systems by actors reinforces the notion that computers are extensions of the human person.[15] In this sense, the ads are not dualistic at all. Good and evil, Mac and PC, man and machine are married in service of the progress myth.

The religion of technology is practiced in the ritual use of technology and the worship of the self that the technologies ultimately foster. In the Greek Narcissus myth, the young man is captivated by his reflection in a pool of water. Marshall McLuhan reminds us that Narcissus was not admiring himself but mistook the reflection in the water for another person. The point of the myth for McLuhan is the fact that "men at once become fascinated by an extension of themselves in any material other than themselves."[16]

The Eastern wisdom traditions seem fitting antidotes for correcting the addiction and narcissism fostered by media technologies. Their emphasis on radical detachment and transcending the self or ego seems a tailor-made response to the temptations of modern technology. But the wisdom traditions themselves have been subsumed by the logic of popular technology and consumerism. The insights of the wisdom tradition are commodified techniques for dealing with the side effects of commodified digital technologies. Participants in the Wisdom 2.0 conference pay upward of $1,500 to learn mindfulness techniques from "the founders of Facebook, Twitter, eBay, Zynga, and PayPal, along with wisdom teachers from various traditions." The top billing at the conference naturally belongs to the technology gurus rather than the spiritual ones.

The confusion of technological values with religious or spiritual ones is a product of a key rhetorical trait shared by both, the paradox. To the nonbeliever, the paradoxes of religion are absurd and irrational diversions. To the true believer, however, they are pathways to enlightenment. Jobs' affinity for paradox in his technological and spiritual thinking may be partly attributed to his "inexhaustible interest in the books of William Blake."[17] The well-worn tale of Jobs' calligraphy class at Reed College being the inspiration for fonts on the Macintosh contains an extremely important detail for reading the techno-religious rhetoric of the Apple mythology. Jobs' professor,

102 Lloyd Reynolds, was an avid reader of William Blake, and was also fascinated by Zen Buddhism. In a course that influenced Jobs profoundly, Reynolds blended these esoteric interests together to articulate a philosophy of life and art that Jobs carried with him.[18] William Blake was an eighteenth-century romantic poet and mystic who, like Jobs, was a multimedia artist who reveled in religious satire. Blake's *The Marriage of Heaven and Hell* was a combination of poems, prose, and illustrations produced on a series of etched plates—an eighteenth-century iPad, if you will. Blake believed that man lost his "Divine Vision," or his ability to see the infinite in all things, because of an overactive intellect. He blamed this loss of vision on Western modes of thinking—an insight Jobs would also adopt after returning from his pilgrimage to India, where he became obsessed with the intuitive abilities of Hindu gurus. Blake was fascinated with Eastern spirituality and owned one of the first English translations of the *Bhagavad Gita*.

In Blake's words, "Without Contraries is no progression. Attraction and Repulsion, Reason and Energy, Love and Hate, are necessary to Human existence." In his *Proverbs of Hell*, Blake presents a series of paradoxes aimed at subverting conventional dualisms: "The road of excess leads to the palace of wisdom,"[19] "You never know what is enough unless you know what is more than enough."[20] Blake's *Marriage of Heaven and Hell* was a critique of the puritanical sentiment sweeping England in the late eighteenth century. Blake used the poem and illustrated plates to subvert traditional dualisms, to propose an alternative cosmology in which good and evil were complementary forces for human flourishing. Heaven represented restraint, while hell represented the creative passions that give humans their joy and energy. The two worked together in harmony to facilitate a more enlightened state of being.

The paradoxes posed by technology are resolved by Jobs in the same spirit. Technology is a powerful medium for creative expression, but absent restraint it has the potential to breed an enslaving addiction. Echoes of Blake's paradoxical style can be heard in the advertising rhetoric of the Apple computer company. Some of the best proverbs come from the company's most iconic campaigns:

- See why 1984 won't be like "1984" (1984 Macintosh)
- While some may see them as the crazy ones, we see genius (1997 "Think Different" campaign)
- Less is more (2003 PowerBook G4)
- Random is the new order (2005 iPod shuffle)
- Touching is believing (2007 iPhone)
- Small is huge (2009 Mac mini)

The iPhone 5 launch in September 2012 announced "The biggest thing to happen to iPhone since iPhone" and "So much more than before. And so much less, too."

Jobs embraced elliptical thinking as a means of promoting technology objects that pose their own paradoxes. In the Apple narrative, the seemingly oppositional notions of assimilation/isolation and freedom/enslavement are resolved by Apple's invocation of enlightened paradox.[21] New media technologies connect us to more people in more places. Marshall McLuhan's "global village" has been invoked more than once to describe the new community that has emerged as a result of networked computing. However, at the same time, mediating relationships from behind a screen breeds a pervasive sense of isolation.

In the Apple story, the brand cult began offline, with users meeting in real, physical locations to swap programs and ideas. Now, the Apple community is more diffuse, concentrated in online discussion groups and support forums. However, Apple product launches and conferences remain sacred pilgrimages where Apple fans can congregate, camp, and live together for days at a time to revel in the communal joy of witnessing the transcendent moment of the new product launch. The reverence once reserved for holy relics and liturgy has reemerged in the technology subculture.

The Apple "1984" advertisement discussed in chapter 1 represents the paradox of freedom and enslavement that technology poses. We might read the cult of drones as the figures in Plato's Allegory of the Cave who have not yet seen the divine light of wisdom and are hypnotized by the shadows on the wall. In Plato's allegory, the images that the prisoners see on the wall are just shadows of reality projected by a hidden light behind them and not reality itself. Plato's allegory still has some relevance today as digital culture places us in the same position as the prisoners. We gaze for hours a day at shadows on the screen. The images we consume are reflections of material reality, but not reality itself. This relationship revives a distinct gnostic sensibility wherein we seek to reveal the secret knowledge that the material world conceals.[22] It is also reminiscent of Blake's concern about the loss of Divine Vision mentioned earlier.

Blake and Jobs were monistic thinkers. Theologically, they viewed the diverse religious traditions as having an essential unity: denominations are manmade separations, they all point to the same God. Jobs said religion was at its best when it emphasized spiritual experiences rather than received dogma. "The juice goes out of Christianity when it becomes too based on faith rather than on living like Jesus or seeing the world as Jesus saw it. . . . I think different religions are different doors to the same house. Sometimes I think the house exists, and sometimes I don't. It's the great mystery."[23]

The culture of digital media provides a shared center of gravity in the information age. The shared experience of living in a highly technological era provides a universal ground for a pluralistic society. There may be many different devices, but only one Internet. Technology has become the new nature—a taken-for-granted order that requires our fidelity. Trappist monk and cultural critic Thomas Merton warned of this new nature:

> The effect of a totally emancipated technology is the regression of man to a climate of moral infancy, in total dependence not on "mother nature" (such a dependence would be partly

tolerable and human) but on the pseudonature of technology, which has replaced nature by a closed system of mechanisms with no purpose but that of keeping themselves going.[24]

Obedience to the new order is expressed in the communication rituals that take place every day in the use of computers, music players, and smartphones—devices that bind individuals together. Media technology presents a paradox though—the absence of presence. The age of electric media is the age of discarnate man—persons communicating without bodies. From the disembodied voice on the telephone to the faceless email message, electronic communication trades human presence for efficiency. The trade-off is not without consequence. Digital media, even "social media," breed detachment, anonymity, and, ironically enough, loneliness. In order for such a form to become popular, it would take a visionary with both technical and humanistic sensibilities; someone to assure the technological faithful that this dramatic change in human relations was a good thing.

Steve Jobs, enigmatic founder of the Apple computer company, was a twenty-first-century corporate hero who oozed an eighteenth-century romantic individualism. Jobs' combination of left brain and right brain genius, his highly developed sense of form and function, and his desire for spiritual enlightenment made him more Leonardo da Vinci than Thomas Edison. To many, Steve Jobs is a true original, but to those who have studied him more closely he is a classic imitator. Jobs was fond of the Picasso quote that good artists borrow and great artists steal. Jobs was a great artist. He ransacked everything from Buddhism to Bauhaus. Jobs' genius was not engineering talent; it was something far more radical. The Renaissance man from Los Altos found a way to imitate God by endowing a cold, lifeless bundle of circuits with a soul.

Much ink has been spilled drafting the Steve Jobs encomium. But Jobs and Apple are interesting for far more than technological prowess—they provide an allegory for reading religion in the information age. Jobs and Apple are further evidence that the shifts in popular

106 religion that occur throughout history are accompanied by changes in the media environment. Digital technology renders us omniscient, omnipresent, and omnipotent. From the farthest satellite to the cell phone in your pocket, the mystical body of electricity connects us all.[25] However, technology is ultimately a false god. From the Tower of Babel to the atomic bomb, man's attempts to apprehend godlike powers often do not end well. The most pervasive tension, the one Jobs spent his life trying to resolve, is that the more we use media technology the more our interior lives shrivel under the artificial glow of the screen. The transformation of perception that accompanies great technological and cultural change has moral consequences. The American transcendentalist Henry David Thoreau foretold as much in *Walden*:

> We must learn to reawaken and keep ourselves awake, not by mechanical aids, but by an infinite expectation of the dawn, which does not forsake us in our soundest sleep. I know of no more encouraging fact than the unquestionable ability of man to elevate his life by a conscious endeavor. It is something to be able to paint a particular picture, or to carve a statue, and so to make a few objects beautiful; but it is far more glorious to carve and paint the very atmosphere and medium through which we look, which morally we can do. To affect the quality of the day, that is the highest of the arts.[26]

Personal technology has become "the very atmosphere and medium" through which we mediate our daily lives. The question that remains is whether this mode of perception brings us any closer to recognizing the transcendent hidden at the heart of that which is not digitized or downloaded.

Notes

Introduction

1   Samantha Murphy, "Apple Store Is NYC Most Photographed Attraction," *Tech-NewsDaily*, May 31, 2011, http://www.technewsdaily.com/2652-apple-store-is -nyc-most-photographed-attraction.html.

2   The phrase "cathedral of consumption" can also be found in George Ritzer, *Enchanting a Disenchanted World: Revolutionizing the Means of Consumption* (Thousand Oaks, Calif.: Sage, 2004) and John Fiske, "Shopping for Pleasure: Malls, Power, and Resistance," in *The Consumer Society Reader*, ed. Juliet B. Schor and Douglas B. Holt (New York: New Press, 2000), 306–28. In the Apple case, consumers are also able to "try on" the products, making the store a "dressing room of consumption"; Julie Marshall, "Interactive Window Shopping: Enchantment in a Rationalized World," *Electronic Journal of Sociology* 1 (2006): 1–12. The rhetoric of consumer enchantment can be traced to Walter Benjamin's theorizing on the Paris arcades in the early twentieth century. See Susan Buck-Morss, *The Dialectics of Seeing: Walter Benjamin and the Arcades Project* (Cambridge, Mass.: MIT Press, 1991).

3   Victor Hugo, *Notre-Dame de Paris*, trans. Isabel F. Hapgood, vol. 7 of *The Works of Victor Hugo* (New York: Kelmscott Society, 1888), 191.

4   For more on the cultural shifts that followed the advent of the printing press, see Elizabeth L. Eisenstein, *The Printing Press as an Agent of Change*, vol. 1

108 (Cambridge: Cambridge University Press, 1980). A discussion of the link between the age of the printing press and the computer age can be found in James A. Dewar, *The Information Age and the Printing Press: Looking Backward to See Ahead* (Santa Monica, Calif.: RAND, 1998). For a more sustained reflection on media, culture, and consciousness, Marshall McLuhan and the media ecology school remain indispensable. See Marshall McLuhan, *The Gutenberg Galaxy* (Toronto: University of Toronto Press, 2012).

5 For more on the cultural interplay between dominant media forms and conceptions of the sacred, see Walter J. Ong, *Orality and Literacy* (New York: Routledge, 2002); Peter G. Horsfield, Mary E. Hess, and Adam M. Medrano, *Belief in Media: Cultural Perspectives on Media and Christianity* (Aldershot: Ashgate, 2004); Stewart M. Hoover and Knut Lundby, eds., *Rethinking Media, Religion, and Culture* (Thousand Oaks, Calif.: Sage, 1997).

6 This appraisal of the sacred function of libraries is taken from Nancy K. Maxwell, *Sacred Stacks: The Higher Purpose of Libraries and Librarianship* (Chicago: American Library Association, 2006).

7 An authoritative discussion of the way in which media and technology forms become metaphors for thought can be found in the media ecology literature, especially in the writings of Marshall McLuhan, Walter Ong, and Neil Postman. See McLuhan, *Understanding Media: The Extensions of Man* (Cambridge, Mass.: MIT Press, 1994); Ong, *Orality and Literacy*; Postman, *Amusing Ourselves to Death: Public Discourse in the Age of Show Business* (New York: Penguin, 2006).

8 The cube and the cathedral comparison was first used by Catholic intellectual George Weigel to describe the growing secularism in Western Europe. See Weigel, *The Cube and the Cathedral: Europe, America, and Politics without God* (New York: Basic Books, 2005).

9 This description combines the insights of Emile Durkheim, Clifford Geertz, and James Carey, who recognize religion as a "cultural system" that promotes a general social order conveying the appearance of implicit fact (Geertz), a set of symbols or things deemed sacred by the community (Durkheim), and a ritual means by which the community constructs, repairs, maintains, and transforms their reality (Carey). See Carey, *Communication as Culture, Revised Edition: Essays on Media and Society* (New York: Taylor & Francis, 2008); Durkheim, *The Elementary Forms of Religious Life*, trans. K. E. Fields (1912; repr., New York: Free Press, 1995); Geertz, *The Interpretation of Cultures* (New York: Basic Books, 1977).

10 The cultural meaning-making process involves a circuit of activities. Scholars in the Birmingham school of cultural studies identify five meaning-making moments in the life of a cultural artifact: production, consumption, identity,

regulation, and representation. The focus of this study is on Apple's advertis- ing images, thus the representation moment of the circuit. For another technology case study that uses this methodology, see Paul du Gay, Stuart Hall, Keith Negus, Hugh Mackay, and Linda Janes, *Doing Cultural Studies: The Story of the Sony Walkman*, vol. 1 (Thousand Oaks, Calif.: Sage, 1997).

11 Advertisements sampled for this book include representative examples from each of the four major product campaigns for Apple: Macintosh (iMac), iPod, iPhone, and iPad. Interested readers can find ads online through Google and YouTube searches, the Coloribus.com advertising database, and sites such as http://www.webdesignerdepot.com/2009/09/the-evolution-of-apple-ads/ and http://www.macmothership.com/gallery/gallerytextindex.html.

12 For more on the history of the parable style in advertising rhetoric, see Roland Marchand, *Advertising the American Dream: Making Way for Modernity, 1920–1940* (Berkeley: University of California Press, 1985), 285–334.

13 Andrew S. Gross, "Cars, Postcards, and Patriotism: Tourism and National Politics in the United States, 1893–1929," *Pacific Coast Philology* 40, no. 1 (2005): 77–97.

14 The use of the term "sublime" can be traced back to Longinus, who used it to refer to great literature. The Kantian sense of the term applies here as it refers to a paradoxical pleasure, one in which the mind is both attracted and repelled by an object for its ability to inspire both wonder and dread. For more on the relationship between the sublime and the natural landscape, see Claudia Bell and John Lyall, *The Accelerated Sublime: Landscape, Tourism, and Identity* (Westport, Conn.: Praeger, 2002).

15 Sociologist of religion Max Weber makes the case that the encroachment of rationalism on all forms of social life, most notably religion, leads to a tear in the social fabric. Individuals are divided by a multitude of value positions that are no longer derived from central institutions but from private rationalization. The result is a disenchantment of religious belief that no longer holds up to the scrutiny of so-called rational analysis. The society that emerges is polytheistic, worshipping not many gods, but many value positions. Weber, *The Protestant Ethic and the Spirit of Capitalism*, trans. Talcott Parsons, foreword by R. H. Tawney (1905; repr., New York: Scribner, 1958).

16 For more on the ways in which Americans have derived a religious feeling from confronting impressive objects like the New York skyline, the Grand Canyon, and the Golden Gate Bridge, see David E. Nye, *American Technological Sublime* (Cambridge, Mass.: MIT Press, 1996).

17 For a discussion of the utopian aspirations and shortcomings associated with the idea of human communication, see John Durham Peters, *Speaking into the Air: A History of the Idea of Communication* (Chicago: University of Chicago Press, 2001), 7.

110 18 Emile Durkheim, *Suicide*, trans. G. Simpson (1897; repr., New York: Free Press, 1951).

19 Sociologist of religion Bryan Wilson writes, "Secularization is in large part intimately involved with the development of technology, since technology is itself the encapsulation of human rationality." Wilson, *Contemporary Transformations of Religion: The Riddell Memorial Lectures, Forty-Fifth Series Delivered at the University of Newcastle Upon Tyne in 1974* (Oxford: Clarendon, 1979), 88.

20 Pui-Yan Lam, "May the Force of the Operating System Be with You: Macintosh Devotion as Implicit Religion," *Sociology of Religion* 62, no. 2 (2001): 243–62.

21 Jesus Martín-Barbero, "Mass Media as a Site of Resacralization of Contemporary Cultures," in Hoover and Lundby, *Rethinking Media, Religion, and Culture*, 112.

22 For a discussion of the ways in which religious value and imagination undergirded art and poetry in the romantic era, see J. Robert Barth, *Romanticism and Transcendence: Wordsworth, Coleridge, and the Religious Imagination* (Columbia: University of Missouri Press, 2003).

23 Bernard M. G. Reardon, *Religion in the Age of Romanticism: Studies in Early Nineteenth Century Thought* (Cambridge: Cambridge University Press, 1985). For a critique of the position that Emerson and Thoreau rejected institutional authority in favor of self-reliance in matters of religion, see Richard A. Grusin, *Transcendentalist Hermeneutics: Institutional Authority and the Higher Criticism of the Bible* (Durham, N.C.: Duke University Press, 1991).

24 Quoted in Carey, *Communication as Culture*, 120.

25 Ursula King, *Teilhard de Chardin and Eastern Religions: Spirituality and Mysticism in an Evolutionary World*, foreword by Joseph Needham (Mahwah, N.J.: Paulist, 2011), 392.

26 Richard Brautigan, *Richard Brautigan's Trout Fishing in America: The Pill Versus the Springhill Mine Disaster; And, In Watermelon Sugar* (Boston: Houghton Mifflin, 1989), 1.

27 For a discussion of the shift away from institutional religion to more subjective religious experiences in the 1960s, see Robert S. Ellwood, *The Sixties Spiritual Awakening* (New Brunswick, N.J.: Rutgers University Press, 1994).

28 Philip Rieff, *The Triumph of the Therapeutic: Uses of Faith after Freud* (Chicago: University of Chicago Press, 1987).

29 Rieff, *Triumph of the Therapeutic*, 236.

30 For a discussion of the way in which new age gurus like Chopra simplify religious, psychological, and sociological insight, secularize it, and package it as a product for "self-actualization," see Jennifer Rindfleish, "Consuming the Self: New Age Spirituality as 'Social Product' in Consumer Society," *Consumption Markets & Culture* 8, no. 4 (2005): 343–60, doi:10.1080/10253860500241930.

For further discussion of "spiritual seeking" in America, see Robert C. Fuller, 111
Spiritual, but Not Religious: Understanding Unchurched America (New York:
Oxford University Press, 2001) and Wade C. Roof, *Spiritual Marketplace: Baby
Boomers and the Remaking of American Religion* (Princeton, N.J.: Princeton
University Press, 2001).

31 Edward Palmer Thompson, *The Making of the English Working Class* (1963;
repr., New York: Penguin, 2002). See also Eric J. Hobsbawm, "The Machine
Breakers," *Past & Present* 1 (1952): 57–70. For further critique of the received
views on Luddism, see Jennifer Daryl Slack and J. Macgregor Wise, *Culture +
Technology: A Primer* (New York: Peter Lang, 2005), 68–74.

32 John A. Heitmann, *The Automobile and American Life* (Jefferson, N.C.:
McFarland, 2009), 26, 88. Heitmann points out that the car had material effects
on religious practice as many churchgoers skipped Sunday service to enjoy the
open road. The author also examines a number of religious criticisms of the automobile that foreshadow the debates that continue today about the relationship
between technology and society.

33 Phoebe S. Kropp, *California Vieja: Culture and Memory in a Modern American
Place* (Berkeley: University of California Press, 2008), 91.

34 Roland Barthes, *Mythologies*, trans. Annette Lavers (1957; repr., New York:
Farrar, Straus & Giroux, 1972), 88. Barthes compares the Citroen automobile
in 1968 to the great Gothic cathedrals, calling them both the "supreme creation"
of their era, consumed by a public that deems them "purely magical" objects.
Michael Bull updates Barthes' essay by including the iPod as another cultural
icon that further mobilizes and privatizes transcendent experience. See Bull,
"Iconic Designs: The Apple iPod," *Senses and Society* 1, no. 1 (2006): 105–8.

35 Michael Moritz, *Return to the Little Kingdom: Steve Jobs, the Creation of Apple,
and How It Changed the World* (New York: Overlook Press, 2009).

36 Marshall McLuhan develops the analogy of electricity being an extension of the
human nervous system in McLuhan, *Understanding Media*.

37 Nicholas Negroponte, *Being Digital* (New York: Knopf Doubleday, 1996).

38 Richard T. Wallis and Jay Bregman, eds., *Neoplatonism and Gnosticism*
(Albany: State University of New York Press, 1992).

39 Michel Foucault, *The Hermeneutics of the Subject: Lectures at the Collège de
France, 1981–1982*, ed. Frédéric Gros, trans. Graham Burchell (New York: Picador, 2005), 211.

40 David Sheff, "Playboy Interview: Steven Jobs," *Playboy*, February 1985, available online at http://www.txtpost.com/playboy-interview-steven-jobs/.

41 Eisenstein, *Printing Press as an Agent of Change*.

42 Tim Berners-Lee, "The World Wide Web and the 'Web of Life' " (1998), http://
www.w3.org/People/Berners-Lee/UU.html.

112 43 An impressive study documenting the decline in civic and religious participation in the age of electronic media can be found in Robert D. Putnam, *Bowling Alone: The Collapse and Revival of American Community* (New York: Simon & Schuster, 2001).

44 Benedict Anderson, *Imagined Communities: Reflections on the Origin and Spread of Nationalism* (London: Verso, 2006).

45 Econsultancy, "The Multi-Screen Marketer" (International Advertising Bureau, May 2012), http://www.iab.net/media/file/The_Multiscreen_Marketer.pdf.

46 Putnam, *Bowling Alone*.

47 Keith Fournier, "Catholics and Worship: As We Worship, so We Believe and so We Live," *Beliefnet*, 2012, http://blog.beliefnet.com/catholicbychoice/2011/02/catholics-and-worship-as-we-worship-so-we-believe-and-so-we-live.html.

48 Sheff, "Playboy Interview: Steven Jobs."

49 For a discussion of the ways in which scientific discourse mimics the rhetoric of religion, see Thomas M. Lessl, "The Culture of Science and the Rhetoric of Scientism: From Francis Bacon to the Darwin Fish," *Quarterly Journal of Speech* 93, no. 2 (2007): 123–49, doi:10.1080/00335630701426785.

50 Gwenfair W. Adams, *Visions in Late Medieval England: Lay Spirituality and Sacred Glimpses of the Hidden Worlds of Faith* (Leiden: Brill, 2007).

51 Umberto Eco, "La bustina di Minerva," *Espresso*, September 30, 1994, excerpts from the English language version available online at http://www.themodern word.com/eco/eco_mac_vs_pc.html. Quotations in the following paragraphs are from this site.

52 Lewis Mumford predates the computer but provides a seminal analysis of the social and cultural effects of the machine age. See Mumford, *Technics and Civilization* (1934; repr., Chicago: University of Chicago Press, 2010). Jacques Ellul issues a warning that also considers the religious implications of a society governed by technology, what he calls *la technique*. See Ellul, *The Technological Society* (New York: Knopf Doubleday, 1980).

53 Paul Messaris, *Visual Persuasion: The Role of Images in Advertising* (Thousand Oaks, Calif.: Sage, 1996).

54 Neil Postman called this the "great symbol drain." See Postman, *Technopoly: The Surrender of Culture to Technology* (New York: Knopf Doubleday, 1993).

Chapter 1

1 Arthur A. Berger, *Narratives in Popular Culture, Media, and Everyday Life* (London: Sage, 1997), 119.

2 Walter Isaacson, "The Genius of Jobs," *New York Times*, October 29, 2011, http://www.nytimes.com/2011/10/30/opinion/sunday/steve-jobss-genius.html?pagewanted=all.

3   For a discussion of the connection between the politics of the Cold War and the
view that technology entraps, endangers, and controls human behavior, see Paul
N. Edwards, *The Closed World: Computers and the Politics of Discourse in Cold
War America* (Cambridge, Mass.: MIT Press, 1997).

4   Sarah Stein makes the case that advertising rhetoric plays a significant role in
the ways in which new technologies are imagined: "The computer revolution
in advanced Western societies insinuates electronic mediation into communica-
tions to an unprecedented degree and increasingly dictates how our social and
economic relationships will be played out. In the absence of public education and
deliberation over the merits and pitfalls of far-reaching technological development, advertising discourses play a crucial role, contributing to expectations of
computer technologies and a sense of identity in relation to them." Stein, "The
'1984' Macintosh Ad: Cinematic Icons and Constitutive Rhetoric in the Launch
of a New Machine," *Quarterly Journal of Speech* 88, no. 2 (2002): 169.

5   The 1984 ad was produced by Chiat/Day and conceived by creative director Lee
Clow, copywriter Steve Hayden, and art director Brent Thomas. The production
budget was $900,000—an unheard-of figure for that time. The ad ran during the
third quarter of Super Bowl XVIII, between the Washington Redskins and the Los
Angeles Raiders.

6   Donna Haraway, "A Cyborg Manifesto," in *The Cultural Studies Reader*, ed.
Simon During, 3rd ed. (London: Routledge, 2007). See also Haraway, "A
Cyborg Manifesto: Science, Technology, and Socialist-Feminism in the Late
Twentieth Century," in *Technology and Values: Essential Readings*, ed. Craig
Hanks, 225–46 (Malden, Mass.: Wiley-Blackwell, 2009).

7   Hans Jonas, *The Gnostic Religion: The Message of the Alien God and the Beginnings of Christianity* (Boston: Beacon, 1958), 80. The excerpt comes from a
scripture of the Peratae in Hippolytus (*Refut.* V.14.1).

8   Wallis and Bregman, *Neoplatonism and Gnosticism*. For more on the relationship between Gnosticism and modern science, see Eric Voegelin, *Science, Politics, and Gnosticism: Two Essays* (Washington, D.C.: Regnery, 1968).

9   *Macheads*, directed by Kobi Shely (Israel: Chimp 65 Productions, 2009), DVD.

10 The most complete treatment of the technology/-icism parallel can be found in
Erik Davis, *TechGnosis: Myth, Magic and Mysticism in the Information Age*
(New York: Crown, 1998).

11 For a historical account of advertising and technology's promotion of self-
actualization as salvation, see T. J. Jackson Lears, "From Salvation to Self-
Realization: Advertising and the Therapeutic Roots of the Consumer Culture,
1880–1930," in *The Culture of Consumption: Critical Essays in American History, 1880–1980*, ed. Richard Wightman Fox and T. J. Jackson Lears, 1–38 (New
York: Pantheon Books, 1983); reprinted in *Advertising & Society Review* 1, no.
1 (2000).

In *Religions of Modernity*, Stef Aupers and Dick Houtman assert that science and technology do not erode the sacred as modern social science tends to suggest; instead they argue via Max Weber and Emile Durkheim that in modernity the sacred is relocated to the self and the digital technologies that act as extensions of the self. Thus, the so-called worship of Apple products is rooted as much in this self-worship as it is in the admiration of the products. Aupers and Houtman, eds., *Religions of Modernity: Relocating the Sacred to the Self and the Digital* (Leiden: Brill, 2010).

12 The ways in which computers become part of our mental life are also taken up in Linda M. Scott, " 'For the Rest of Us': A Reader-Oriented Interpretation of Apple's '1984' Commercial," *Journal of Popular Culture* 25, no. 1 (1991): 67–81. See also Georges Poulet, "Criticism and the Experience of Interiority," in *Reader-Response Criticism: From Formalism to Post-structuralism*, ed. Jane P. Tompkins (Baltimore: Johns Hopkins University Press, 1980), 43.

13 Alan Kay, "User Interface: A Personal View," in *The Art of Human-Computer Interface Design*, ed. Brenda Laurel (New York: Addison-Wesley, 1990), 193.

14 The commercial was released in 1997 and was directed by Jennifer Golub from Chiat/Day agency. Richard Dreyfuss did the voiceover, although an alternative version was made with Steve Jobs performing the voiceover. The Steve Jobs version never aired. The television ad earned a 1998 Emmy Award and a 2000 Effie Award for most effective campaign in America.

15 For a discussion of the way in which the "Think Different" ad fit the fin de siècle mood at the end of the millennium, see Ronald E. Shields, "The Force of Callas' Kiss: The 1997 Apple Advertising Campaign, 'Think Different,' " *Text and Performance Quarterly* 21, no. 3 (2001): 202–19.

16 Walter Isaacson, *Steve Jobs* (New York: Simon & Schuster, 2011), 119.

17 Isaacson, *Steve Jobs*.

18 Isaacson, *Steve Jobs*, 48–49.

19 Susan Giesemann North, "Are the Barbarians of Technology Knocking at the Gate? Vico and Scientism in Twentieth-Century Culture," in *Rhetoric, the Polis, and the Global Village: Selected Papers from the 1998 Thirtieth Anniversary Rhetoric Society of America Conference*, ed. C. Jan Swearingen and David S. Kaufer (Mahwah, N.J.: Lawrence Erlbaum, 1999). Giesemann North mentions the "Think Different" ad as an example of the Cartesian solipsism that has taken root in the modern age. Echoing Giambattista Vico, an eighteenth-century Italian professor of rhetoric, Giesemann North shows the ways in which the technological society amplifies solipsism and skepticism, disposing men to follow their own senses rather than uniting in a common truth. Beyond tapping into cultural values of individuality and creativity and the ethos of the cultural figures represented, the "Think Different" ad presents a troubling bit of logic. If we are called

to "think different" and the Apple computer helps us do so, "what will serve to facilitate communication, cooperation or a sense of community between and among all these differently thinking individuals?" (178).

20 Gráinne M. Fitzsimons, Tanya L. Chartrand, and Gavan J. Fitzsimons, "Automatic Effects of Brand Exposure on Motivated Behavior: How Apple Makes You 'Think Different,'" *Journal of Consumer Research* 35, no. 1 (2008): 21–35. Advertising's ability to create brand personalities has also worked in reverse. Our personalities are often shaped by the brands with which we associate. In consumer behavior experiments, individuals shown an Apple logo tended to behave more creatively than those shown logos from other companies like IBM.

21 Annette W. Balkema and Henk Slager, *Exploding Aesthetics*, vol. 16 (Amsterdam: Rodopi, 2001), 146.

22 George Lakoff and Mark Johnson, "The Metaphorical Structure of the Human Conceptual System," *Cognitive Science* 4, no. 2 (1980): 195–208, doi:10.1207/s15516709cog0402_4. Cognitive science holds that the human conceptual system is fundamentally metaphorical. In other words, the way we talk about thinking involves using metaphors. For example, the concept "idea" can be a person, as in "cognitive psychology is in its infancy," or a plant, "that idea has not yet come to fruition," or food, "I just can't swallow that claim." The source of such metaphors is the language itself, or it can be those universal aspects of human existence that give shape and form to otherwise abstract concepts. Computer technology provides its own stock of thinking metaphors: "I cannot process all that information," or the more tongue-in-cheek "I think, therefore iMac."

23 According to those familiar with Jobs' involvement with the iMac print campaign, Jobs penned the "I think, therefore iMac" line himself; see Bradley Johnson, "Jobs Orchestrates Ad Blitz for Apple's New iMac PC," *Advertising Age*, August 10, 1998.

24 For a discussion of nostalgia appeals in advertising rhetoric, see Barbara B. Stern, "Historical and Personal Nostalgia in Advertising Text: The Fin de Siècle Effect," *Journal of Advertising* 21, no. 4 (1992): 11–22.

25 The iMac G4, released in 2001, featured a swivel arm that connected a half-dome base to a flat-screen monitor.

26 Elizabeth Outka, *Consuming Traditions: Modernity, Modernism, and the Commodified Authentic*, vol. 1 (New York: Oxford University Press, 2008).

27 Buck-Morss, *Dialectics of Seeing*, 83.

28 The use of nostalgic signifiers is one way in which brand narratives can be rendered allegorical. See Stephen Brown, Robert V. Kozinets, and John F. Sherry Jr., "Teaching Old Brands New Tricks: Retro Branding and the Revival of Brand Meaning," *Journal of Marketing* 67, no. 3 (2003): 19–33.

29 David Gruber, "From the Screen to Me, 1984–2008," *Media History* 16, no. 3

(2010): 341–56. Gruber argues that human-computer interaction has been imagined in a series of phases since the advent of the personal computer: disembodied cyberspace where no humans are shown in ads, embodied hybridity where we see humans working with computers, and ubiquity where no machines are shown. Ubiquity is characterized by recent computer ads in which the machines are not shown at all (see the "Get a Mac" analysis in this chapter). Gruber's typology is helpful in mapping the metaphorical personification of technology. His conclusion that technology has become increasingly invisible as it blends into our everyday practices is worth noting as technology's epistemic effects become less obvious. A notable exception to Gruber's categorization is the Apple "1984" ad, in which no computers are shown and human actors are used to dramatize the ideological battle between Apple and conformity. In this sense, Apple's prophetic "1984" ad foreshadowed the coming age of computer ubiquity.

30   Marshall McLuhan put it this way: "It is this continuous embrace of our own technology in daily use that puts us in the Narcissus role of subliminal awareness and numbness in relation to these images of ourselves. By continuously embracing technologies, we relate ourselves to them as servomechanisms. That is why we must, to use them at all, serve these objects, these extensions of ourselves, as gods or minor religions." For further discussion, see McLuhan, *Understanding Media*, 46.

31   For further discussion about the psychological link between humans and computers, see Sherry Turkle, *The Second Self* (New York: Simon & Schuster, 1984). Turkle argues that computers change not only what we do but also how we think. This psychological shift is largely "invisible" in that shifts in "how we think" require a certain level of "metacognition" or thinking about thinking. Monitoring the brain's own activity is also a feature of Zen Buddhism—a practice with which Jobs was quite familiar. The various references to thinking in the Apple discourse, including "Think Different" and "I think, therefore iMac," reflect a preoccupation with the ways in which computers both mimic and influence cognition.

32   "The birth or coming to life of the machine is not simply the product of a rational, scientific design; it is not simply a matter of construction, of putting parts together, of engineering. Rather such a machine is necessarily infused with a living spirit, with a soul; it is a 'dead' technological object reanimated, given the status of an autonomous subject. This bringing to life of technology must obviously, then, take place as much through magical or spiritual means as through science." Randolph L. Rutsky, *High Techne: Art and Technology from the Machine Aesthetic to the Posthuman*, vol. 2 (Minneapolis: University of Minnesota Press, 1999), 24.

33   McLuhan, *Understanding Media*, 8.

34 For a discussion of the recursive relationship between humans and the technologi-
    cal environment, see Andy Clark, *Natural-Born Cyborgs: Minds, Technologies,
    and the Future of Human Intelligence* (New York: Oxford University Press, 2004),
    11. "It is the mind-body scaffolding problem. It is the problem of understanding
    how human thought and reason is born out of looping interactions between mate-
    rial brains, material bodies, and complex cultural and technological environments.
    We create these supportive environments, but they create us too. We exist, as the
    thinking things we are, only thanks to a baffling dance of brains, bodies, and cul-
    tural and technological scaffolding."

35 Another scholar who has dealt with identity and the "Get a Mac" campaign is
    Randall Livingstone, "Better at Life Stuff: Consumption, Identity, and Class in
    Apple's 'Get a Mac' Campaign," *Journal of Communication Inquiry* 35, no. 3
    (2011): 210–34. Livingstone argues that Apple is skilled at promoting the myth
    of self-actualization through commodification.

36 Sherry Turkle, *Life on the Screen: Identity in the Age of the Internet* (New York:
    Simon & Schuster, 1997), 129.

37 Turkle, *Life on the Screen*, 129.

38 Josef Pieper, *Leisure: The Basis of Culture and the Philosophical Act* (San Fran-
    cisco: Ignatius, 2009), 15.

39 Pieper, *Leisure*, 15.

Chapter 2

*   This chapter is a significantly revised version of an essay that first appeared
    in *Drugs and Media: New Perspectives on Communication, Consumption and
    Consciousness*, ed. Robert C. MacDougall (London: Continuum, 2012), 123–42.

1   Chloe Albanesius, "Apple Unveils Updated iPod Nano, Touch," *PC Magazine*,
    October 4, 2011, http://www.pcmag.com/article2/0,2817,2394061,00.asp.

2   Steven Levy, "iPod Nation," *Newsweek*, July 26, 2004, 42.

3   Donald Melanson, "Apple: 16 Billion iTunes Songs Downloaded, 300 Million
    iPods Sold," *Engadget*, October 4, 2011, http://www.engadget.com/2011/10/04/
    apple-16-billion-itunes-songs-downloaded-300-million-ipods-sol.

4   Stephen Evans, "Apple a Day Keeps the Music at Play," *BBC*, April 21,
    2005, http://news.bbc.co.uk/2/hi/programmes/from_our_own_correspondent/
    4464735.stm.

5   Michael Bull, *Sound Moves: iPod Culture and Urban Experience* (New York:
    Taylor & Francis, 2008), 151.

6   Bull, *Sound Moves*, 46.

7   Leander Kahney, *The Cult of Mac* (San Francisco: No Starch Press, 2006).

8   Kahney, *Cult of Mac*, 3.

9   Bull, *Sound Moves*, 151.

118 10 Stefan Lorenz Sorgner and Oliver Fürbeth, eds., *Music in German Philosophy: An Introduction*, trans. Susan H. Gillespie, intro. to the English ed. by Michael Spitzer, and foreword by H. James Birx (Chicago: University of Chicago Press, 2011).

11 Thomas Carlyle, *Thomas Carlyle's Works: Critical and Miscellaneous Essays* (London: Chapman & Hall, 1888), 509.

12 Walter Pater, *The Renaissance: Studies in Art and Poetry* (Berkeley: University of California Press, 1980), 64.

13 Ken Segall, *Insanely Simple: The Obsession That Drives Apple's Success* (New York: Penguin, 2012).

14 Segall, *Insanely Simple*.

15 Segall, *Insanely Simple*.

16 Isaacson, *Steve Jobs*.

17 Tricia Sheffield provides a broad survey of this topic that draws heavily from the sociology of religion developed by Durkheim. Sheffield argues that "advertising, in the guise of divine mediator and consumer sacrament, helps mediate ultimate concern, which communicates to the individual the objects of value in the culture of consumer capitalism. . . . [A]dvertising is best understood through a totemic lens, in that totems mark a group of people as a specific consumer community." Sheffield, *The Religious Dimensions of Advertising* (New York: Palgrave Macmillan, 2006), xii.

18 For further discussion of the analogy among advertising, art, and religion, see Judith Williamson, *Decoding Advertisements: Ideology and Meaning in Advertising* (London: Marion Boyars, 1978); Sut Jhally, *The Codes of Advertising: Fetishism and the Political Economy of Meaning in the Consumer Society* (New York: Taylor & Francis, 1990); James B. Twitchell, *Adcult USA: The Triumph of Advertising in American Culture* (New York: Columbia University Press, 1996). While Williamson and Jhally employ a Marxist critique, Twitchell is more of an apologist for advertising and its "religious" function in consumer society.

19 Thomas M. Lessl, "Toward a Definition of Religious Communication: Scientific and Religious Uses of Evolution," *Journal of Communication and Religion* 16, no. 2 (1993): 127–38.

20 For more on iPod advertising as symbolical realism and iconic hypostasis, see Eric Jenkins, "My iPod, My iCon: How and Why Do Images Become Icons?" *Critical Studies in Media Communication* 25, no. 5 (2008): 466–89.

21 Kenneth J. Gergen, "The Challenge of Absent Presence," in *Perpetual Contact: Mobile Communication, Private Talk, Public Performance*, ed. James E. Katz and Mark Aakhus (Cambridge: Cambridge University Press, 2002), 227.

22 John Edgar Tidwell and Cheryl R. Ragar, eds., *Montage of a Dream: The Art and Life of Langston Hughes*, foreword by Arnold Rampersad (Columbia: University of Missouri Press, 2007), 271.

23 Leander Kahney, *The Cult of iPod* (San Francisco: No Starch Press, 2005).

24 Hailing comes from Judith Williamson's interpretive treatment of print advertising that relies on Louis Althusser's concept of "appellation." In Althusser's conception, appellation is the way ideology works, by summoning us (consumers) with a "hey you," as if the ad were intended for the viewer personally. The "Hey Mama" song of the original iPod ad may be interpreted as a more sexist expression of Althusser's "hey you" appellation. See Williamson, *Decoding Advertisements*.

25 The title of this section is taken from a C. S. Lewis novel of the same name; the novel is a retelling of the Greek myth of Cupid and Psyche.

26 Gary Edson, *Masks and Masking: Faces of Tradition and Belief Worldwide* (Jefferson, N.C.: McFarland, 2005).

27 David Wiles, *Mask and Performance in Greek Tragedy: From Ancient Festival to Modern Experimentation* (Cambridge: Cambridge University Press, 2007).

28 Lewis Mumford, *Technics and Human Development: The Myth of the Machine* (Boston: Houghton Mifflin Harcourt, 1967).

29 Todd Gitlin, *Media Unlimited, Revised Edition: How the Torrent of Images and Sounds Overwhelms Our Lives* (London: Picador, 2007), 119.

30 Quoted in Michael Bull, *Sounding Out the City: Personal Stereos and the Management of Everyday Life* (Oxford: Berg, 2000), 136.

31 Quoted in Michele Hannoosh, *Baudelaire and Caricature: From the Comic to an Art of Modernity* (University Park: Pennsylvania State University Press, 1992), 299.

32 The flaneur, French for stroller or loafer, is the idle urban explorer who leisurely enjoys the enchantment of the city streets. The iPod adds another aesthetic layer to the strolling experience, a personalized soundtrack. For more on the flaneur, see Charles Baudelaire, *The Painter of Modern Life* (London: Penguin, 2010).

33 Isabel Pedersen, " 'No Apple iPhone? You Must Be Canadian': Mobile Technologies, Participatory Culture, and Rhetorical Transformation," *Canadian Journal of Communication* 33, no. 3 (2008): 491–510.

34 Adriano Sack and Ingo Niermann, *The Curious World of Drugs and Their Friends: A Very Trippy Miscellany*, trans. Amy Patton (New York: Penguin, 2008), 57.

35 Timothy Leary, *Turn On, Tune In, Drop Out* (Berkeley, Calif.: Ronin, 1999), 147.

36 Quoted in Mark Dery, *Escape Velocity: Cyberculture at the End of the Century* (New York: Grove, 1997), 28.

37 Quoted in Graham S. John, *Rave Culture and Religion* (New York: Taylor & Francis, 2003), 157.

38 Bethina Liu, "Lab Crosses Boundaries," *Harvard Crimson*, May 12, 2010, http://www.thecrimson.com/article/2010/5/12/lab-dance-science-ayogu/.

39 Jacques Ellul, quoted in Davis, *TechGnosis*, 205.

Chapter 3

1 Ron Rosenbaum, "Secrets of the Little Blue Box," *Esquire Magazine*, October 1971, 76, 117–25, 222.

2 Brian Lam, "The Pope Says Worship Not False iDols: Save Us, Oh True Jesus Phone," *Gizmodo*, December 26, 2006, http://gizmodo.com/gadgets/cellphones/the-pope-says-worship-not-false-idols-save-us-oh-true-jesus-phone-224143.php.

3 Pope Benedict XVI, "'Urbi et Orbi' Message of His Holiness Pope Benedict XVI," December 25, 2006, http://www.vatican.va/holy_father/benedict_xvi/messages/urbi/documents/hf_ben-xvi_mes_20061225_urbi_en.html.

4 David Noble argues that Christian concepts of perfection and impending apocalypse are dangerous ideas for framing the agenda of science and technology. For more on the intermingling of technological progress and transcendent desire, see Noble, *The Religion of Technology: The Divinity of Man and the Spirit of Invention* (New York: Penguin, 1999).

5 Lam, "Pope Says Worship Not False iDols."

6 Heidi A. Campbell and Antonio C. La Pastina, "How the iPhone Became Divine: New Media, Religion and the Intertextual Circulation of Meaning," *New Media & Society* 12, no. 7 (2010): 1191–1207. Campbell and La Pastina identify the intertextual strategies used by Apple and the popular media to perpetuate the religious rhetoric associated with the iPhone. The analysis in this chapter builds upon the work of Campbell and La Pastina by suggesting that the iPhone rhetoric does not merely recirculate religious symbols and ideas; it also articulates a particular set of ultimate concerns about living in the digital age.

7 Neil Postman calls this the "great symbol drain," a condition that strips symbols of sacred or traditional meaning and trivializes them for the purpose of shock or entertainment value. Postman, *Technopoly*.

8 Clifford Geertz noted, "Symbol systems, man created, shared, conventional, ordered and indeed learned, provide human beings with a meaningful framework for orienting themselves to one another, to the world around them, and to themselves. At once a product and a determinant of social interaction, they are to the process of social life as a computer's program is to its operation." Ultimately, Geertz modified this conception because it did not account for the dialectic between the "pattern of meaning" and the "concrete course of social life." In other words, Geertz believed cultural meaning was always in flux because the symbolic patterns that define culture are also always being renegotiated. The dynamism of everyday life feeds the symbol system with new material and reconfigures the old. It is telling, though, that the metaphor of the computer program is invoked as a way to understand patterns of meaning creation. Geertz, *Interpretation of Cultures*, 250.

9 Fredric Jameson, *Postmodernism, or, The Cultural Logic of Late Capitalism* 121
(Durham, N.C.: Duke University Press, 1990), 80.

10 Andrew Benjamin, *The Lyotard Reader* (Malden, Mass.: Wiley-Blackwell,
1991).

11 The "technological sublime" first appeared in Perry Miller, *The Life of the Mind
in America: Books One through Three* (Orlando, Fla.: Harcourt, Brace & World,
1965). Leo Marx's landmark work on the "rhetoric of the technological sublime" provides an example of American studies work that has traced the spiritual
rhetoric of technology observers during the industrial age. Marx, *The Machine in
the Garden: Technology and the Pastoral Ideal in America* (New York: Oxford
University Press, 2000). David Nye builds on Miller and Marx and makes a case
for the way in which awe-inspiring new technologies provide a sense of unity
and common purpose, becoming a de facto religion. Nye, *American Technological Sublime*.

12 Nye, *American Technological Sublime*, 13.

13 The headlines surrounding the Y2K computer problem in 1999 are indicative
of the pseudo-religious rhetoric surrounding the potential collapse of modern
technology. For more on this topic, see Karen Pärna, "Digital Apocalypse: The
Implicit Religiosity of the Millennium Bug Scare," in Aupers and Houtman,
Religions of Modernity, 239.

14 The ad's allusion to "doubting Thomas" and the creation myth is also explored
in Campbell and La Pastina, "How the iPhone Became Divine." This book adds
to the work of Campbell and La Pastina by suggesting that the Apple rhetoric
recirculates religious symbols, conveys an implicit set of cultural values, and
critiques surrounding new technology adoption and use.

15 Roland Barthes, *Image-Music-Text*, trans. Stephen Heath (New York: Farrar,
Straus & Giroux, 1978). Barthes explains that text in an image works as linguistic anchor, assisting the reader in choosing the right level of perception and
pointing the reader toward the correct details to notice. When Barthes was writing in the 1960s, text was still featured prominently in advertisements. The bal-
ance has shifted in contemporary advertising as text is now overshadowed by
image, if there is any text at all. In this configuration, the image provides clues to
solve the riddle of the text, rather than the other way around. See Charles Forceville, *Pictorial Metaphor in Advertising* (New York: Taylor & Francis, 1998).

16 Modern critics are more apt to critique this "ocularcentrism." Martin Jay contends
that the renewed interest in hermeneutics is an attempt to crack the ideological
code obfuscated by the proliferation of images. Celebrated iconoclast Jacques
Ellul provides a prototypical critique of vision as antihistorical because it lacks
the successive temporality of language as a means of discovering truth. This
current of antivisual discourse in contemporary philosophy of communication

might view Apple's penchant for lush iconography and sensual immersion as a blatant attempt at nurturing idolatry, the enemy of iconoclasm. For an authoritative survey of the prominent critics of ocularcentrism, see Jay, *Downcast Eyes: The Denigration of Vision in Twentieth-Century French Thought* (Berkeley: University of California Press, 1993).

17 Kenneth Burke, *The Rhetoric of Religion: Studies in Logology* (Berkeley: University of California Press, 1970), 170–71.

18 The creation myth is not constrained to the iPhone image. It is also present in the Apple subculture, a grouping of dedicated consumers so loyal to the Apple brand that they have been referred to as a cult. Belk and Tumbat detected several religious myths at work among Apple followers: a creation myth (the company starting in a garage), a messianic myth (visionary founder Steve Jobs), a satanic myth (Apple's competition with IBM/Windows), and a resurrection myth (the return of Steve Jobs). These narratives are said to play a significant role in the construction of the Apple cult's identity. While this approach is illustrative of one of the ways in which technology can be understood as mythos, it is ahistorical. The authors interpret the responses of a diverse group of Apple brand community members as Judeo-Christian clichés rather than addressing the question of why media technology attracts such religious allusion. The answer to such a question lies in the fact that media technology objectifies an essential human social practice, communication, by which culture and belief are ultimately created and maintained. For more on this topic, see Russell W. Belk and Gulnur Tumbat, "The Cult of Macintosh," *Consumption Markets & Culture* 8, no. 3 (2005): 205–17.

19 The term "technological mysticism" is developed further in William A. Stahl, *God and the Chip: Religion and the Culture of Technology* (Waterloo, Ont.: Wilfrid Laurier University Press, 1999), 13. The concept refers to mankind's "faith in the universal efficacy of technology."

20 Horsfield, Hess, and Medrano, *Belief in Media*, xv–xvii. For more on the relationship disenchantment wrought by rationalism, see Stephen Toulmin, *Cosmopolis: The Hidden Agenda of Modernity* (Chicago: University of Chicago Press, 1992).

21 The Wiccan religion and other new age movements demonstrate the modern tendency to see religion itself as a technology—something to be mastered as both art and science. See Elisabeth Arweck and William J. F. Keenan, *Materializing Religion: Expression, Performance and Ritual* (Aldershot: Ashgate, 2006). The concurrent development of the computer culture and the popularization of pagan and new age religious ideas begs some interesting questions. Both emerged from the foment of the 1960s, and many of the leading figures in computer research and development, including Steve Jobs, were new age devotees.

22 Max Weber's "Science as a Vocation," quoted in Aupers and Houtman, *Religions of Modernity*, 1.

23 Psychiatrist Robert W. Daly calls this quasi-supernatural power and agency of technology the "spectre of technology." See Bronislaw Szerszynski, *Nature, Technology and the Sacred* (Malden, Mass.: Wiley-Blackwell, 2008), 63. Szerszynski argues that the sublimity of technology can lead to a disconnect between the development of technologies and their "fitness for human life and purpose" (63). The result is that technology becomes loved for itself—a modern form of idolatry.

24 David Pogue, "New iPhone Conceals Sheer Magic," *New York Times*, October 11, 2011, http://www.nytimes.com/2011/10/12/technology/personaltech/iphone-4s-conceals-sheer-magic-pogue.html?_r=2andpagewanted=1.

25 Ellul, *Technological Society*, 131.

26 Ellul, *Technological Society*, 131.

27 Alex Cocotas, "Chart: More Than 30 Billion Apps Have Been Downloaded in the App Store," *Business Insider*, August 23, 2012, http://www.businessinsider.com/more-than-30-billion-apps-have-been-downloaded-in-the-app-store-2012-8.

28 Apple website, http://www.apple.com/iphone/from-the-app-store/.

29 Scholars who have investigated the religiosity of the Apple brand community include Belk and Tumbat, "Cult of Macintosh"; and Albert M. Muñiz Jr. and Hope J. Schau, "Religiosity in the Abandoned Apple Newton Brand Community," *Journal of Consumer Research* 31, no. 4 (2005): 737–47.

30 See Noble, *Religion of Technology*.

31 Paul Virilio expands Einstein's phrase in his theoretical work, *The Information Bomb*. Virilio's critique warns against the perils of science and technology without conscience. The acceleration brought about by global communication and information technology creates the conditions for a catastrophic accident. Virilio uses the Asian stock market crash of the late 1990s as an example (one that would turn out to be prophetic in light of the impending crash of the world financial markets half a decade later). Virilio, *The Information Bomb*, vol. 10 (London: Verso Books, 2006).

32 Paul Virilio, *Virilio Live: Selected Interviews*, ed. John Armitage (Thousand Oaks, Calif.: Sage, 2001), 44.

33 Quoted in Paramahansa Yogananda, *Autobiography of a Yogi* (New York: Sterling, 2003), 226.

Chapter 4

1 David Sheff, "The Night Steve Jobs Met Andy Warhol," *Playboy*, January 2012, http://davidsheff.com/Remembering_Steve_Jobs.html.

2 On technology and mysticism, Erik Davis writes, "The logic of technology has

124   become invisible—literally occult. Without the code you're mystified. And no
         one has all the codes anymore." The esoteric nature of computer programming
         and development feeds the popular mythologies and iconographies that depict
         the machine as something transcendent, magical, and mysterious. Davis, *Tech-Gnosis*, 181.

3   Jim Collins points out that the postmodern character of Western society is not
         a result of the new replacing the old but the way in which the old gets recycled
         together with the new. "The ever-expanding number of texts and technologies
         is both a reflection and a significant contribution to the 'array'—the perpetual
         circulation and recirculation of signs that forms the fabric of postmodern life."
         Collins, *Film Theory Goes to the Movies: Cultural Analysis of Contemporary
         Film* (New York: Routledge, 1992).

4   Ellul, *Technological Society*, 142.

5   Marshall McLuhan adopted Ezra Pound's claim that artists are the "antennae
         of the race" to describe the way in which artists are able to foretell the sensory
         adaptations required by a changing technological environment. "Art as radar acts
         as an 'early alarm system,' as it were, enabling us to discover social and psychic
         targets in lots of time to prepare to cope with them. This concept of the arts as
         prophetic contrasts with the popular idea of them as mere self-expression. If an
         art is an 'early warning system,' to use the phrase from World War II, when radar
         was new, art has the utmost relevance not only to media study but to the devel-
         opment of media controls." McLuhan, *Understanding Media*, xi. For more on
         McLuhan's theoretical elaborations see Donald F. Theall, *The Virtual Marshall
         McLuhan* (Montreal: McGill-Queen's University Press, 2001).

6   Ezra Pound, *Literary Essays of Ezra Pound*, ed. T. S. Eliot (New York: New
         Directions, 1968), 297.

7   Richard B. Kershner, *Cultural Studies of James Joyce* (Amsterdam: Rodopi,
         2003). Literary critic Wyndham Lewis accused Joyce of trying to "transform
         the living into the machine." Lewis, *Time and Western Man*, ed. Paul Edwards
         (Santa Rosa, Calif.: Black Sparrow Press, 1993), 91–92.

8   McLuhan's interpretation of Pound can be found in Elena Lamberti, *Marshall
         McLuhan's Mosaic: Probing the Literary Origins of Media Studies* (Toronto:
         University of Toronto Press, 2012). For further discussion on technology and
         transcendence in art, see J. Sage Elwell, *Crisis of Transcendence: A Theology of
         Digital Art and Culture* (Lanham, Md.: Lexington Books, 2011).

9   Walter Benjamin, *The Work of Art in the Age of Mechanical Reproduction* (New
         York: Penguin, 2008).

10   Sheff, "Playboy Interview: Steven Jobs."

11   Alexis de Tocqueville, *Democracy in America*, vols. 1 and 2, trans. H. Reeve
         (1838; repr., Stilwell, Kans.: Digireads.com, 2007), 325.

12 Jane D. Dillenberger, *The Religious Art of Andy Warhol* (London: Bloomsbury, 125 2001), 33.

13 Paul Giles, *Roman Catholicism in American Literature: Ideology and Aesthetics* (Cambridge: Cambridge University Press, 1992), 281.

14 Robert Pincus-Witten, "Pre-entry: Margins of Error," *Arts Magazine* 63, no. 1 (1989): 58.

15 Quoted in Michael S. Malone, *Infinite Loop: How the World's Most Insanely Great Computer Company Went Insane* (New York: Currency/Doubleday, 1999), 15.

16 Malone, *Infinite Loop*, 15.

17 Malone, *Infinite Loop*, 15.

18 Jeffrey S. Young and William L. Simon, *iCon: Steve Jobs, the Greatest Second Act in the History of Business* (Hoboken, N.J.: Wiley, 2005).

19 Young and Simon, *iCon*, 25.

20 Young and Simon, *iCon*, 31.

21 Young and Simon, *iCon*, 32.

22 Jeffrey L. Cruikshank, *The Apple Way: Twelve Management Lessons from the World's Most Innovative Company* (New York: McGraw-Hill, 2005), 91.

23 Cruikshank, *Apple Way*, 99.

24 Young and Simon, *iCon*.

25 Isaacson, *Steve Jobs*, 527.

26 Yogananda, *Autobiography of a Yogi*, 279.

27 Yogananda, *Autobiography of a Yogi*, 159.

28 Jay Stevens, *Storming Heaven: LSD and the American Dream* (New York: Grove/Atlantic, 1998).

29 Baba Ram Dass, *Be Here Now* (New York: Crown, 1971), 15.

Conclusion

* American Progress, 1872 (oil on canvas), Gast, John (fl. 1872) / Private Collection / Photo © Christie's Images/The Bridgeman Art Library.

1 Frederick Merk and Lois B. Merk, *Manifest Destiny and Mission in American History: A Reinterpretation* (Cambridge, Mass.: Harvard University Press, 1963).

2 Daniel W. Howe, *What Hath God Wrought: The Transformation of America, 1815–1848* (New York: Oxford University Press, 2007).

3 Jeffrey Sconce, *Haunted Media: Electronic Presence from Telegraphy to Television* (Durham, N.C.: Duke University Press, 2000), 22.

4 Quoted in Tom Wolfe, *Hooking Up* (London: Picador, 2001), 74.

126   5   Online Etymology Dictionary (2012), http://www.etymonline.com/index.php? term=religion.

6   Xerox's famous miscalculation was immortalized in Douglas K. Smith and Robert C. Alexander, *Fumbling the Future: How Xerox Invented, Then Ignored, the First Personal Computer* (New York: William Morrow, 1988).

7   Ong, *Orality and Literacy*, 98–101.

8   This thesis is argued from a media ecology perspective in Peter K. Fallon, *The Metaphysics of Media: Toward an End of Postmodern Cynicism and the Construction of a Virtuous Reality* (Scranton, Pa.: University of Scranton Press, 2010).

9   Postman, *Technopoly*, 4. Postman argues that the Egyptian myth found in Plato's *Phaedrus* dialogue is a call for a more circumspect appraisal of our own technological society.

10   Postman, *Technopoly*, 4.

11   Shane Hipps, *The Hidden Power of Electronic Culture: How Media Shapes Faith, the Gospel, and Church* (Grand Rapids: Zondervan, 2006), 27. Hipps gives Neil Postman credit for the Faustian bargain metaphor as it pertains to modern technology.

12   Matt Richtel, "Silicon Valley Says Step Away from the Device," *New York Times*, July 23, 2012, http://www.nytimes.com/2012/07/24/technology/silicon-valley-worries-about-addiction-to-devices.html?pagewanted=all.

13   Wisdom 2.0 (2012), http://www.wisdom2summit.com/.

14   Isaacson, *Steve Jobs*, 50.

15   McLuhan, *Understanding Media*.

16   Gary Genosko, *Marshall McLuhan: Renaissance for a Wired World* (New York: Routledge, 2005), 97.

17   Harriet Rubin, "C.E.O. Libraries Reveal Keys to Success," *New York Times*, July 21, 2007, http://www.nytimes.com/2007/07/21/business/21libraries.html.

18   Henry Adams, "A Tribute to a Great Artist: Steve Jobs," *Smithsonian*, October 6, 2011, http://www.smithsonianmag.com/arts-culture/A-Tribute-to-a-Great-Artist--Steve-Jobs.html.

19   William Blake, *The Complete Poetry and Prose of William Blake*, ed. David V. Erdman (Berkeley: University of California Press, 2008), 35.

20   Blake, *Complete Poetry*, 37.

21   David Glen Mick and Susan Fournier, "Paradoxes of Technology: Consumer Cognizance, Emotions, and Coping Strategies," *The Journal of Consumer Research* 25, no. 2 (1998): 123–43.

22   Davis, *TechGnosis*.

23   Isaacson, *Steve Jobs*, 15.

24 Thomas Merton, *Conjectures of a Guilty Bystander* (New York: Doubleday,
1968), 71.

25 Marshall McLuhan, Eric McLuhan, and Jacek Szklarek, *The Medium and the Light: Reflections on Religion* (Eugene, Ore.: Wipf & Stock, 2010). McLuhan suggests the connectivity afforded by electricity is a metaphorical facsimile of the mystical body of Christ; in effect, an antichrist.

26 Henry David Thoreau, *Walden* (Boston: Houghton Mifflin, 1894), 142.

Credits

The following groups and individuals are gratefully acknowledged for images included in this book: SeanPavonePhoto, Keith Levit, and Dmitriy Yakovlev (Shutterstock), Jonathan Hordle (Rex/Rex USA), Atoma (Wikipedia—CC Attribution ShareAlike 2.5 license), Mark Hillary and Sonia Fantoli (Flickr—CC Attribution 2.0 Generic license), Roberto Parada, Christie's Images/The Bridgeman Art Library, and Margaret Bourke-White/Masters/Getty Images. Andy Warhol works © 2013 The Andy Warhol Foundation for the Visual Arts, Inc. / Artists Rights Society (ARS), New York; additional rights for Warhol's "Apple Macintosh" from Ronald Feldman Fine Arts, New York / www.feldmangallery .com.

Bibliography

Adams, Gwenfair W. *Visions in Late Medieval England: Lay Spiritual-ity and Sacred Glimpses of the Hidden Worlds of Faith*. Leiden: Brill, 2007.

Adams, Henry. "A Tribute to a Great Artist: Steve Jobs." *Smithsonian*, October 6, 2011. http://www.smithsonianmag.com/arts-culture/A -Tribute-to-a-Great-Artist--Steve-Jobs.html.

Albanesius, Chloe. "Apple Unveils Updated iPod Nano, Touch." *PC Magazine*, October 4, 2011. http://www.pcmag.com/article2/0 ,2817,2394061,00.asp.

Anderson, Benedict. *Imagined Communities: Reflections on the Origin and Spread of Nationalism*. London: Verso, 2006.

Arweck, Elisabeth, and William J. F. Keenan. *Materializing Religion: Expression, Performance and Ritual*. Aldershot: Ashgate, 2006.

Aupers, Stef, and Dick Houtman, eds. *Religions of Modernity: Relocat-ing the Sacred to the Self and the Digital*. Leiden: Brill, 2010.

Balkema, Annette W., and Henk Slager. *Exploding Aesthetics*. Vol. 16. Amsterdam: Rodopi, 2001.

Barth, J. Robert. *Romanticism and Transcendence: Wordsworth,*

130   *Coleridge, and the Religious Imagination.* Columbia: University of Missouri Press, 2003.

Barthes, Roland. *Image-Music-Text.* Translated by Stephen Heath. New York: Farrar, Straus & Giroux, 1978.

———. *Mythologies.* Translated by Annette Lavers. 1957. Reprint, New York: Farrar, Straus & Giroux, 1972.

Baudelaire, Charles. *The Painter of Modern Life.* London: Penguin, 2010.

Belk, Russell W., and Gulnur Tumbat. "The Cult of Macintosh." *Consumption Markets & Culture* 8, no. 3 (2005): 205–17.

Bell, Claudia, and John Lyall. *The Accelerated Sublime: Landscape, Tourism, and Identity.* Westport, Conn.: Praeger, 2002.

Benjamin, Andrew. *The Lyotard Reader.* Malden, Mass.: Wiley-Blackwell, 1991.

Benjamin, Walter. *The Work of Art in the Age of Mechanical Reproduction.* New York: Penguin, 2008.

Berger, Arthur A. *Narratives in Popular Culture, Media, and Everyday Life.* London: Sage, 1997.

Berners-Lee, Tim. "The World Wide Web and the 'Web of Life.'" 1998. http://www.w3.org/People/Berners-Lee/UU.html.

Blake, William. *The Complete Poetry and Prose of William Blake.* Edited by David V. Erdman. Berkeley: University of California Press, 2008.

Brautigan, Richard. *Richard Brautigan's Trout Fishing in America: The Pill Versus the Springhill Mine Disaster; And, In Watermelon Sugar.* Boston: Houghton Mifflin, 1989.

Brown, Stephen, Robert V. Kozinets, and John F. Sherry Jr. "Teaching Old Brands New Tricks: Retro Branding and the Revival of Brand Meaning." *Journal of Marketing* 67, no. 3 (2003): 19–33.

Buck-Morss, Susan. *The Dialectics of Seeing: Walter Benjamin and the Arcades Project.* Cambridge, Mass.: MIT Press, 1991.

Bull, Michael. "Iconic Designs: The Apple iPod." *Senses and Society* 1, no. 1 (2006): 105–8.

———. *Sound Moves: iPod Culture and Urban Experience.* New York: Taylor & Francis, 2008.

———. *Sounding Out the City: Personal Stereos and the Management of Everyday Life.* Oxford: Berg, 2000.

Burke, Kenneth. *The Rhetoric of Religion: Studies in Logology.* Berke- ley: University of California Press, 1970.

Campbell, Heidi A., and Antonio C. La Pastina. "How the iPhone Became Divine: New Media, Religion and the Intertextual Circulation of Meaning." *New Media & Society* 12, no. 7 (2010): 1191–1207.

Carey, James W. *Communication as Culture, Revised Edition: Essays on Media and Society.* New York: Taylor & Francis, 2008.

Carlyle, Thomas. *Thomas Carlyle's Works: Critical and Miscellaneous Essays.* London: Chapman & Hall, 1888.

Clark, Andy. *Natural-Born Cyborgs: Minds, Technologies, and the Future of Human Intelligence.* New York: Oxford University Press, 2004.

Cocotas, Alex. "Chart: More Than 30 Billion Apps Have Been Downloaded in the App Store." *Business Insider*, August 23, 2012. http://www.businessinsider.com/more-than-30-billion-apps-have-been-downloaded-in-the-app-store-2012-8.

Collins, Jim. *Film Theory Goes to the Movies: Cultural Analysis of Contemporary Film.* New York: Routledge, 1992.

Cruikshank, Jeffrey L. *The Apple Way: Twelve Management Lessons from the World's Most Innovative Company.* New York: McGraw-Hill, 2005.

Dass, Baba Ram. *Be Here Now.* New York: Crown, 1971.

Davis, Erik. *TechGnosis: Myth, Magic and Mysticism in the Information Age.* New York: Crown, 1998.

de Tocqueville, Alexis. *Democracy in America.* Vols. 1 and 2. Translated by H. Reeve. 1838. Reprint, Stilwell, Kans.: Digireads.com, 2007.

Dery, Mark. *Escape Velocity: Cyberculture at the End of the Century.* New York: Grove, 1997.

Dewar, James A. *The Information Age and the Printing Press: Looking Backward to See Ahead.* Santa Monica, Calif.: RAND, 1998.

Dillenberger, Jane D. *The Religious Art of Andy Warhol.* London: Bloomsbury, 2001.

Du Gay, Paul, Stuart Hall, Keith Negus, Hugh Mackay, and Linda Janes. *Doing Cultural Studies: The Story of the Sony Walkman.* Vol. 1. Thousand Oaks, Calif.: Sage, 1997.

132 Durkheim, Emile. *The Elementary Forms of Religious Life.* Translated by K. E. Fields. 1912. Reprint, New York: Free Press, 1995.

———. *Suicide.* Translated by G. Simpson. 1897. Reprint, New York: Free Press, 1951.

Eco, Umberto. "La bustina di Minerva." *Espresso,* September 30, 1994. Excerpts from the English language version available online at http://www.themodernword.com/eco/eco_mac_vs_pc.html.

Econsultancy. "The Multi-Screen Marketer." International Advertising Bureau, May 2012. http://www.iab.net/media/file/The_Multiscreen_Marketer.pdf.

Edson, Gary. *Masks and Masking: Faces of Tradition and Belief Worldwide.* Jefferson, N.C.: McFarland, 2005.

Edwards, Paul N. *The Closed World: Computers and the Politics of Discourse in Cold War America.* Cambridge, Mass.: MIT Press, 1997.

Eisenstein, Elizabeth L. *The Printing Press as an Agent of Change.* Vol. 1. Cambridge: Cambridge University Press, 1980.

Ellul, Jacques. *The Technological Society.* New York: Knopf Doubleday, 1980.

Ellwood, Robert S. *The Sixties Spiritual Awakening.* New Brunswick, N.J.: Rutgers University Press, 1994.

Elwell, J. Sage. *Crisis of Transcendence: A Theology of Digital Art and Culture.* Lanham, Md.: Lexington Books, 2011.

Evans, Stephen. "Apple a Day Keeps the Music at Play." *BBC,* April 21, 2005. http://news.bbc.co.uk/2/hi/programmes/from_our_own_correspondent/4464735.stm.

Fallon, Peter K. *The Metaphysics of Media: Toward an End of Postmodern Cynicism and the Construction of a Virtuous Reality.* Scranton, Pa.: University of Scranton Press, 2010.

Fiske, John. "Shopping for Pleasure: Malls, Power, and Resistance." In *The Consumer Society Reader,* edited by Juliet B. Schor and Douglas B. Holt, 306–28. New York: New Press, 2000.

Fitzsimons, Gráinne M., Tanya L. Chartrand, and Gavan J. Fitzsimons. "Automatic Effects of Brand Exposure on Motivated Behavior: How Apple Makes You 'Think Different.'" *Journal of Consumer Research* 35, no. 1 (2008): 21–35.

Forceville, Charles. *Pictorial Metaphor in Advertising.* New York: Taylor & Francis, 1998.

Foucault, Michel. *The Hermeneutics of the Subject: Lectures at the Collège de France, 1981–1982.* Edited by Frédéric Gros. Translated by Graham Burchell. New York: Picador, 2005.

Fournier, Keith. "Catholics and Worship: As We Worship, so We Believe and so We Live." *Beliefnet,* 2012. http://blog.beliefnet. com/catholicbychoice/2011/02/catholics-and-worship-as-we -worship-so-we-believe-and-so-we-live.html.

Fuller, Robert C. *Spiritual, but Not Religious: Understanding Unchurched America.* New York: Oxford University Press, 2001.

Geertz, Clifford. *The Interpretation of Cultures.* New York: Basic Books, 1977.

Giesemann North, Susan. "Are the Barbarians of Technology Knocking at the Gate? Vico and Scientism in Twentieth-Century Culture." In Swearingen and Kaufer, *Rhetoric, the Polis, and the Global Village,* 175–82.

Genosko, Gary. *Marshall McLuhan: Renaissance for a Wired World.* New York: Routledge, 2005.

Gergen, Kenneth J. "The Challenge of Absent Presence." In *Perpetual Contact: Mobile Communication, Private Talk, Public Performance,* edited by James E. Katz and Mark Aakhus, 227–41. Cambridge: Cambridge University Press, 2002.

Giles, Paul. *American Catholic Arts and Fictions: Culture, Ideology, Aesthetics.* Cambridge: Cambridge University Press, 1992.

———. *Roman Catholicism in American Literature: Ideology and Aesthetics.* Cambridge: Cambridge University Press, 1992.

Gitlin, Todd. *Media Unlimited, Revised Edition: How the Torrent of Images and Sounds Overwhelms Our Lives.* London: Picador, 2007.

Gross, Andrew S. "Cars, Postcards, and Patriotism: Tourism and National Politics in the United States, 1893–1929." *Pacific Coast Philology* 40, no. 1 (2005): 77–97.

Gruber, David. "From the Screen to Me, 1984–2008." *Media History* 16, no. 3 (2010): 341–56.

Grusin, Richard A. *Transcendentalist Hermeneutics: Institutional Authority and the Higher Criticism of the Bible.* Durham, N.C.: Duke University Press, 1991.

134 Guinness, Os. *The Call: Finding and Fulfilling the Central Purpose of Your Life.* Nashville: Thomas Nelson, 2003.

Hackforth, Reginald. *Plato: Phaedrus.* Cambridge: Cambridge University Press, 1972.

Hannoosh, Michele. *Baudelaire and Caricature: From the Comic to an Art of Modernity.* University Park: Pennsylvania State University Press, 1992.

Haraway, Donna. "A Cyborg Manifesto." In *The Cultural Studies Reader,* edited by Simon During, 3rd ed. (London: Routledge, 2007).

————. "A Cyborg Manifesto: Science, Technology, and Socialist-Feminism in the Late Twentieth Century." In *Technology and Values: Essential Readings,* edited by Craig Hanks, 225–46. Malden, Mass.: Wiley-Blackwell, 2009.

Heitmann, John A. *The Automobile and American Life.* Jefferson, N.C.: McFarland, 2009.

Hipps, Shane. *The Hidden Power of Electronic Culture: How Media Shapes Faith, the Gospel, and Church.* Grand Rapids: Zondervan, 2006.

Hobsbawm, Eric J. "The Machine Breakers." *Past & Present* 1 (1952): 57–70.

Hoover, Stewart M., and Knut Lundby, eds. *Rethinking Media, Religion, and Culture.* Thousand Oaks, Calif.: Sage, 1997.

Horsfield, Peter G., Mary E. Hess, and Adan M. Medrano. *Belief in Media: Cultural Perspectives on Media and Christianity.* Aldershot: Ashgate, 2004.

Howe, Daniel W. *What Hath God Wrought: The Transformation of America, 1815–1848.* New York: Oxford University Press, 2007.

Hugo, Victor. *Notre-Dame de Paris.* Vol. 7 of *The Works of Victor Hugo.* Translated by Isabel F. Hapgood. New York: Kelmscott Society, 1888.

Isaacson, Walter. "The Genius of Jobs." *New York Times,* October 29, 2011. http://www.nytimes.com/2011/10/30/opinion/sunday/steve-jobss-genius.html?pagewanted=all.

————. *Steve Jobs.* New York: Simon & Schuster, 2011.

Jameson, Fredric. *Postmodernism, or, The Cultural Logic of Late Capitalism.* Durham, N.C.: Duke University Press, 1990.

Jay, Martin. *Downcast Eyes: The Denigration of Vision in Twentieth-* 135
Century French Thought. Berkeley: University of California Press, 1993.

Jenkins, Eric. "My iPod, My iCon: How and Why Do Images Become Icons?" *Critical Studies in Media Communication* 25, no. 5 (2008): 466–89.

Jhally, Sut. *The Codes of Advertising: Fetishism and the Political Economy of Meaning in the Consumer Society.* New York: Taylor & Francis, 1990.

John, Graham S. *Rave Culture and Religion.* New York: Taylor & Francis, 2003.

Johnson, Bradley. "Jobs Orchestrates Ad Blitz for Apple's New iMac PC." *Advertising Age*, August 10, 1998.

Jonas, Hans. *The Gnostic Religion: The Message of the Alien God and the Beginnings of Christianity.* Boston: Beacon, 1958.

Jung, Carl G. *Psychology and Religion.* New Haven, Conn.: Yale University Press, 1960.

Kahney, Leander. *The Cult of iPod.* San Francisco: No Starch Press, 2005.

———. *The Cult of Mac.* San Francisco: No Starch Press, 2006.

Kavoori, Anandam P., and Noah Arceneaux. *The Cell Phone Reader: Essays in Social Transformation.* New York: Peter Lang, 2006.

Kay, Alan. "User Interface: A Personal View." In *The Art of Human-Computer Interface Design*, edited by Brenda Laurel, 191–207. New York: Addison-Wesley, 1990.

Kershner, Richard B. *Cultural Studies of James Joyce.* Amsterdam: Rodopi, 2003.

King, Ursula. *Teilhard de Chardin and Eastern Religions: Spirituality and Mysticism in an Evolutionary World.* Foreword by Joseph Needham. Mahwah, N.J.: Paulist Press, 2011.

Kropp, Phoebe S. *California Vieja: Culture and Memory in a Modern American Place.* Berkeley: University of California Press, 2008.

Lakoff, George, and Mark Johnson. "The Metaphorical Structure of the Human Conceptual System." *Cognitive Science* 4, no. 2 (1980): 195–208. doi:10.1207/s15516709cog0402_4.

Lam, Brian. "The Pope Says Worship Not False iDols: Save Us, Oh True Jesus Phone." *Gizmodo*, December 26, 2006. http://gizmodo.

136 com/gadgets/cellphones/the-pope-says-worship-not-false-idols
-save-us-oh-true-jesus-phone-224143.php.

Lam, Pui-Yan. "May the Force of the Operating System Be with You: Macintosh Devotion as Implicit Religion." *Sociology of Religion* 62, no. 2 (2001): 243–62.

Lamberti, Elena. *Marshall McLuhan's Mosaic: Probing the Literary Origins of Media Studies.* Toronto: University of Toronto Press, 2012.

Lears, T. J. Jackson. "From Salvation to Self-Realization: Advertising and the Therapeutic Roots of the Consumer Culture, 1880–1930." In *The Culture of Consumption: Critical Essays in American History, 1880–1980,* edited by Richard Wightman Fox and T. J. Jackson Lears, 1–38. New York: Pantheon Books, 1983. Reprinted in *Advertising & Society Review* 1, no. 1 (2000).

Leary, Timothy. *Turn On, Tune In, Drop Out.* Berkeley, Calif.: Ronin, 1999.

Lessl, Thomas M. "The Culture of Science and the Rhetoric of Scientism: From Francis Bacon to the Darwin Fish." *Quarterly Journal of Speech* 93, no. 2 (2007): 123–49. doi:10.1080/00335630701426785.

———. "Toward a Definition of Religious Communication: Scientific and Religious Uses of Evolution." *Journal of Communication and Religion* 16, no. 2 (1993): 127–38.

Levy, Steven. "iPod Nation." *Newsweek,* July 26, 2004, 42.

Lewis, Wyndham. *Time and Western Man.* Edited by Paul Edwards. Santa Rosa, Calif.: Black Sparrow Press, 1993.

Liu, Bethina. "Lab Crosses Boundaries." *Harvard Crimson,* May 12, 2010. http://www.thecrimson.com/article/2010/5/12/lab-dance-science-ayogu/.

Livingstone, Randall. "Better at Life Stuff: Consumption, Identity, and Class in Apple's 'Get a Mac' Campaign." *Journal of Communication Inquiry* 35, no. 3 (2011): 210–34.

Macheads. Directed by Kobi Shely. Israel: Chimp 65 Productions, 2009. DVD.

Malone, Michael S. *Infinite Loop: How the World's Most Insanely Great Computer Company Went Insane.* New York: Currency/Doubleday, 1999.

Marchand, Roland. *Advertising the American Dream: Making Way for* 137 *Modernity, 1920–1940.* Berkeley: University of California Press, 1985.

Marshall, Julie. "Interactive Window Shopping: Enchantment in a Rationalized World." *Electronic Journal of Sociology* 1 (2006): 1–12.

Martín-Barbero, Jesus. "Mass Media as a Site of Resacralization of Contemporary Cultures." In Hoover and Lundby, *Rethinking Media, Religion, and Culture*, 102–16.

Marx, Leo. *The Machine in the Garden: Technology and the Pastoral Ideal in America.* New York: Oxford University Press, 2000.

Maxwell, Nancy K. *Sacred Stacks: The Higher Purpose of Libraries and Librarianship.* Chicago: American Library Association, 2006.

McLuhan, Marshall. *The Gutenberg Galaxy.* Toronto: University of Toronto Press, 2012.

———. "Myth and Mass Media." *Daedalus* 88, no. 2 (1959): 339–48.

———. *Understanding Media: The Extensions of Man.* Cambridge, Mass.: MIT Press, 1994.

McLuhan, Marshall, Eric McLuhan, and Jacek Szklarek. *The Medium and the Light: Reflections on Religion.* Eugene, Ore.: Wipf & Stock, 2010.

Melanson, Donald. "Apple: 16 Billion iTunes Songs Downloaded, 300 Million iPods Sold." *Engadget*, October 4, 2011. http://www.engadget.com/2011/10/04/apple-16-billion -itunes-songs-downloaded-300-million-ipods-sol.

Merk, Frederick, and Lois B. Merk. *Manifest Destiny and Mission in American History: A Reinterpretation.* Cambridge, Mass.: Harvard University Press, 1963.

Merton, Thomas. *Conjectures of a Guilty Bystander.* New York: Doubleday, 1968.

Messaris, Paul. *Visual Persuasion: The Role of Images in Advertising.* Thousand Oaks, Calif.: Sage, 1996.

Mick, David Glen, and Susan Fournier. "Paradoxes of Technology: Consumer Cognizance, Emotions, and Coping Strategies." *The Journal of Consumer Research* 25, no. 2 (1998): 123–43.

Miller, Perry. *The Life of the Mind in America: Books One through Three.* Orlando, Fla.: Harcourt, Brace & World, 1965.

138   Moritz, Michael. *Return to the Little Kingdom: Steve Jobs, the Creation of Apple, and How It Changed the World.* New York: Overlook Press, 2009.

Mumford, Lewis. *Technics and Civilization.* 1934. Reprint, Chicago: University of Chicago Press, 2010.

———. *Technics and Human Development: The Myth of the Machine.* Boston: Houghton Mifflin Harcourt, 1967.

Muñiz, Albert M., Jr., and Hope J. Schau. "Religiosity in the Abandoned Apple Newton Brand Community." *Journal of Consumer Research* 31, no. 4 (2005): 737–47.

Murphy, Samantha. "Apple Store Is NYC Most Photographed Attraction." *TechNewsDaily*, May 31, 2011. http://www.technewsdaily. com/2652-apple-store-is-nyc-most-photographed-attraction.html.

Negroponte, Nicholas. *Being Digital.* New York: Knopf Doubleday, 1996.

Noble, David F. *The Religion of Technology: The Divinity of Man and the Spirit of Invention.* New York: Penguin, 1999.

Nye, David E. *American Technological Sublime.* Cambridge, Mass.: MIT Press, 1996.

Ong, Walter J. *Orality and Literacy.* New York: Routledge, 2002.

Online Etymology Dictionary. 2012. http://www.etymonline.com/index .php?term=religion.

Outka, Elizabeth. *Consuming Traditions: Modernity, Modernism, and the Commodified Authentic.* Vol. 1. New York: Oxford University Press, 2008.

Pärna, Karen. "Digital Apocalypse: The Implicit Religiosity of the Millennium Bug Scare." In Aupers and Houtman, *Religions of Modernity*, 239–60.

Pater, Walter. *The Renaissance: Studies in Art and Poetry.* Berkeley: University of California Press, 1980.

Pedersen, Isabel. " 'No Apple iPhone? You Must Be Canadian': Mobile Technologies, Participatory Culture, and Rhetorical Transformation." *Canadian Journal of Communication* 33, no. 3 (2008): 491–510.

Peters, John Durham. *Speaking into the Air: A History of the Idea of Communication.* Chicago: University of Chicago Press, 2001.

Pieper, Josef. *Leisure: The Basis of Culture and the Philosophical Act.*
San Francisco: Ignatius, 2009.

Pincus-Witten, Robert. "Pre-entry: Margins of Error." *Arts Magazine* 63, no. 10 (1989): 58.

Pogue, David. "New iPhone Conceals Sheer Magic." *New York Times,* October 11, 2011. http://www.nytimes.com/2011/10/12/technology/personaltech/iphone-4s-conceals-sheer-magic-pogue.html?_r=2andpagewanted=1.

Pope Benedict XVI. " 'Urbi et Orbi' Message of His Holiness Pope Benedict XVI." December 25, 2006. http://www.vatican.va/holy_father/benedict_xvi/messages/urbi/documents/hf_ben-xvi_mes_200 61225_urbi_en.html.

Postman, Neil. *Amusing Ourselves to Death: Public Discourse in the Age of Show Business.* New York: Penguin, 2006.

———. *Technopoly: The Surrender of Culture to Technology.* New York: Knopf Doubleday, 1993.

Poulet, Georges. "Criticism and the Experience of Interiority." In *Reader-Response Criticism: From Formalism to Post-structuralism,* edited by Jane P. Tompkins, 41–49. Baltimore: Johns Hopkins University Press, 1980.

Pound, Ezra. *Literary Essays of Ezra Pound.* Edited by T. S. Eliot. New York: New Directions, 1968.

Putnam, Robert D. *Bowling Alone: The Collapse and Revival of American Community.* New York: Simon & Schuster, 2001.

Reardon, Bernard M. G. *Religion in the Age of Romanticism: Studies in Early Nineteenth Century Thought.* Cambridge: Cambridge University Press, 1985.

Richtel, Matt. "Silicon Valley Says Step Away from the Device." *New York Times,* July 23, 2012. http://www.nytimes.com/2012/07/24/technology/silicon-valley-worries-about-addiction-to-devices.html?pagewanted=all.

Rieff, Philip. *The Triumph of the Therapeutic: Uses of Faith after Freud.* Chicago: University of Chicago Press, 1987.

Rindfleish, Jennifer. "Consuming the Self: New Age Spirituality as 'Social Product' in Consumer Society." *Consumption Markets & Culture* 8, no. 4 (2005): 343–60. doi:10.1080/10253860500241930.

140 Ritzer, George. *Enchanting a Disenchanted World: Revolutionizing the Means of Consumption.* Thousand Oaks, Calif.: Sage, 2004.

Roof, Wade C. *Spiritual Marketplace: Baby Boomers and the Remaking of American Religion.* Princeton, N.J.: Princeton University Press, 2001.

Rosenbaum, Ron. "Secrets of the Little Blue Box." *Esquire Magazine,* October 1971, 76, 117–25, 222.

Rubin, Harriet. "C.E.O. Libraries Reveal Keys to Success." *New York Times,* July 21, 2007. http://www.nytimes.com/2007/07/21/business/21libraries.html.

Rutsky, Randolph L. *High Techne: Art and Technology from the Machine Aesthetic to the Posthuman.* Vol. 2. Minneapolis: University of Minnesota Press, 1999.

Sack, Adriano, and Ingo Niermann. *The Curious World of Drugs and Their Friends: A Very Trippy Miscellany.* Translated by Amy Patton. New York: Penguin, 2008.

Sconce, Jeffrey. *Haunted Media: Electronic Presence from Telegraphy to Television.* Durham, N.C.: Duke University Press, 2000.

Scott, Linda M. " 'For the Rest of Us': A Reader-Oriented Interpretation of Apple's '1984' Commercial." *Journal of Popular Culture* 25, no. 1 (1991): 67–81.

Segall, Ken. *Insanely Simple: The Obsession That Drives Apple's Success.* New York: Penguin, 2012.

Sheff, David. "The Night Steve Jobs Met Andy Warhol." *Playboy,* January 2012. http://davidsheff.com/Remembering_Steve_Jobs.html.

———. "Playboy Interview: Steven Jobs." *Playboy,* February 1985. Available online at http://www.txtpost.com/playboy-interview-steven-jobs/.

Sheffield, Tricia. *The Religious Dimensions of Advertising.* New York: Palgrave Macmillan, 2006.

Shields, Ronald E. "The Force of Callas' Kiss: The 1997 Apple Advertising Campaign, 'Think Different.' " *Text and Performance Quarterly* 21, no. 3 (2001): 202–19.

Slack, Jennifer Daryl, and J. Macgregor Wise. *Culture + Technology: A Primer.* New York: Peter Lang, 2005.

Smith, Douglas K., and Robert C. Alexander. *Fumbling the Future:*
How Xerox Invented, Then Ignored, the First Personal Computer.
New York: William Morrow, 1988.

Sorgner, Stefan Lorenz, and Oliver Fürbeth, eds. *Music in German Philosophy: An Introduction.* Translated by Susan H. Gillespie, introduction to the English ed. by Michael Spitzer, and foreword by H.
James Birx. Chicago: University of Chicago Press, 2011.

Stahl, William A. *God and the Chip: Religion and the Culture of Technology.* Waterloo, Ont.: Wilfrid Laurier University Press, 1999.

Stein, Sarah R. "The '1984' Macintosh Ad: Cinematic Icons and Constitutive Rhetoric in the Launch of a New Machine." *Quarterly
Journal of Speech* 88, no. 2 (2002): 169–92.

Stern, Barbara B. "Historical and Personal Nostalgia in Advertising
Text: The Fin de Siècle Effect." *Journal of Advertising* 21, no. 4
(1992): 11–22.

————. "Other-Speak: Classical Allegory and Contemporary Advertising." *Journal of Advertising* 19, no. 3 (1990): 14–26.

Stevens, Jay. *Storming Heaven: LSD and the American Dream.* New
York: Grove/Atlantic, 1998.

Swearingen, C. Jan, and David S. Kaufer, eds. *Rhetoric, the Polis, and
the Global Village: Selected Papers from the 1998 Thirtieth Anniversary Rhetoric Society of America Conference.* Mahwah, N.J.:
Lawrence Erlbaum, 1999.

Szerszynski, Bronislaw. *Nature, Technology and the Sacred.* Malden,
Mass.: Wiley-Blackwell, 2008.

Theall, Donald F. *The Virtual Marshall McLuhan.* Montreal: McGill-
Queen's University Press, 2001.

Thompson, Edward Palmer. *The Making of the English Working Class.*
1963. Reprint, New York: Penguin, 2002.

Thoreau, Henry David. *Walden.* Boston: Houghton Mifflin, 1894.

Tidwell, John Edgar, and Cheryl R. Ragar, eds. *Montage of a Dream:
The Art and Life of Langston Hughes.* Foreword by Arnold Rampersad. Columbia: University of Missouri Press, 2007.

Toulmin, Stephen. *Cosmopolis: The Hidden Agenda of Modernity.* Chicago: University of Chicago Press, 1992.

Turkle, Sherry. *Life on the Screen: Identity in the Age of the Internet.*
New York: Simon & Schuster, 1997.

142 ———. *The Second Self.* New York: Simon & Schuster, 1984.

Twitchell, James B. *Adcult USA: The Triumph of Advertising in American Culture.* New York: Columbia University Press, 1996.

Virilio, Paul. *The Information Bomb.* Vol. 10. London: Verso Books, 2006.

———. *Virilio Live: Selected Interviews.* Edited by John Armitage. Thousand Oaks, Calif.: Sage, 2001.

Voegelin, Eric. *Science, Politics, and Gnosticism: Two Essays.* Washington, D.C.: Regnery, 1968.

Wallis, Richard T., and Jay Bregman, eds. *Neoplatonism and Gnosticism.* Albany: State University of New York Press, 1992.

Weber, Max. *The Protestant Ethic and the Spirit of Capitalism.* Translated by Talcott Parsons, with a foreword by R. H. Tawney. 1905. Reprint, New York: Scribner, 1958.

Weigel, George. *The Cube and the Cathedral: Europe, America, and Politics without God.* New York: Basic Books, 2005.

Wiles, David. *Mask and Performance in Greek Tragedy: From Ancient Festival to Modern Experimentation.* Cambridge: Cambridge University Press, 2007.

Williamson, Judith. *Decoding Advertisements: Ideology and Meaning in Advertising.* London: Marion Boyars, 1978.

Wilson, Bryan. *Contemporary Transformations of Religion: The Riddell Memorial Lectures, Forty-Fifth Series Delivered at the University of Newcastle Upon Tyne in 1974.* Oxford: Clarendon, 1979.

Wisdom 2.0. 2012. http://www.wisdom2summit.com/.

Wolfe, Tom. *Hooking Up.* London: Picador, 2001.

Yogananda, Paramahansa. *Autobiography of a Yogi.* New York: Sterling, 2003.

Young, Jeffrey S., and William L. Simon. *iCon: Steve Jobs, the Greatest Second Act in the History of Business.* Hoboken, N.J.: Wiley, 2005.

Index

Index

Index